How to Manage Your Career

How to Manage Your Career

The Power of Mindset in Fostering Success

Kelly Swingler

BEP BUSINESS EXPERT PRESS

How to Manage Your Career: The Power of Mindset in Fostering Success

Copyright © Business Expert Press, LLC, 2017.

First published in 2017 by
Business Expert Press, LLC
222 East 46th Street, New York, NY 10017
www.businessexpertpress.com

ISBN-13: 978-1-94709-800-8 (paperback)
ISBN-13: 978-1-94709-801-5 (e-book)

Business Expert Press Human Resource Management and Organizational Behavior Collection

Collection ISSN: 1946-5637 (print)
Collection ISSN: 1946-5645 (electronic)

Cover and interior design by Exeter Premedia Services Private Ltd., Chennai, India

First edition: 2017

10 9 8 7 6 5 4 3 2 1

Printed in the United States of America.

Abstract

If you are looking to move to the next level of your career then this book is for you. The author has written an easy-to-understand, easy-to-digest book about mindset that includes the neuroscience about why we think and feel the way we do, hints and tips on how to take control of and grow your own career, and case studies, hints, tips, and tools to help you manage your career through the power of mindset to help you foster success.

You will learn what mindset is, understand growth and fixed mindsets, and discover how to gain a different perspective into everyday workplace and life occurrences and how just some simple yet effective mindset shifts can make the difference between stagnation and growth.

Kelly Swingler, Founder of Chrysalis Consulting, has been working with mindset for years and her techniques and insights helped her own career where she was recruited as the UK's youngest HR Director while being mum to twin boys, and is now running one of the leading HR Consultancies in the UK, with an emphasis on doing things differently.

Kelly and her clients have benefitted from understanding and implementing mindset techniques to help them foster success in their careers and get to the next level, and you can too.

This book is dedicated to all those who want to master their mindset.

Keywords

action, beliefs, career, change, mindset, positive action, positive interaction, positive thinking, success, thoughts

Contents

Acknowledgments

I've been on an amazing journey since writing my first book *Create Your Purpose and Manage Your Time* and could probably write an entire book just based on who to thank for their support in the creation of *How to Manage Your Career: The Power of Mindset in Fostering Success*; so if I have missed you out, I sincerely apologize.

Thank you, first of all, to my Mum for being so open and honest over recent months and confirming that our own beliefs are key to our happiness.

To Callum and Robert, who do not have a clue what I do, but who have listened to me anyway and who have grown into amazing young men with their own minds and their own beliefs.

To my Dad for growing old disgracefully and being consistent in attitude and actions.

To my brother and sister for being true to themselves and following their own paths.

My angels who have been there every step of the way for guidance, advice, wine (and soft drinks), food, and pixie dust.

The amazing team at Chrysalis Consulting who have kept driving and striving for greatness and working hard whilst my butterfly mind comes up with one crazy idea after another, and a special thanks to Peter for your endless kind words and support.

My family and friends for accepting me as me, madness and all.

To Cameron for taking an interest in everything and to Harry.

Bowser for your endless walks to help me clear my head.

And finally, thanks to my amazing partner Mick for keeping me focused and grounded—you are my absolute rock and I am lucky to have you as my partner in business and life.

Introduction

Without even realizing it, I have been working on and with mindset for years.

Always fascinated by why we do or think certain things and why animals don't act in the same way.

As a child I was fixated by the language and behaviors of others, often wondering why from my bedroom window I could see children as young as five smoking cigarettes they had stolen from family members. Why some of the kids I went to school with chose a path of crime, and why I wanted to achieve as much as I could in my career.

As a teenager I was fascinated with television programs and books about serial killers, not so much the crimes, but why they would have done what they did in the first place and why they were different from most of society. The views of the psychologists, journalists, and writers were always interesting as they were "certain" about why acts had taken place.

The books such as *Ugly* and *Anorexic* about abuse, neglect, and self-hatred are also fascinating as the victim realizes they have a choice, and when they realize they have choices, they are able to turn their lives around quickly and for the better.

Watching the Tyson versus Bruno fight with friends in my teens and seeing the difference in the fighters as they walked into the ring, knowing that Tyson would win because he clearly wanted it more, much to the annoyance of everyone I was with.

Seeing in my sons, my family, friends, and in myself that if the belief is that something can't be done, it's not going to be done.

Watching athletes from a variety of sports win when they had the right mindset, attitude, and belief.

Throughout my HR career I was constantly looking at people and why they said and did things. What possesses someone to take action that results in them being disciplined? Surely people don't come to work thinking "I'm going to give really poor service today."!

Events and the actions of others can of course impact us, but everything we do, say, and believe stems from choice and beliefs, and the influence of this comes from our mindset.

We each have a choice—every day of our lives we have a choice. If we wake up and think it's going to be a rubbish day, it's going to be a rubbish day. If we think it's going to be a good day, it generally is.

Stuff gets in the way, life gets in the way, and while we are in control of our own thoughts and actions, we aren't in control of the thoughts and actions of others, and sometimes external influences impact us—that's life and we need to deal with it. If we are in the right mindset, we deal with obstacles much better and in a much more innovative and logical way.

When I became a mum my mindset shifted from my somewhat selfish views and onto wanting and needing to provide for my sons. Lack of rest and severe PND (postnatal depression) were a struggle, but my house was clean, my sons were well looked after, and my career was still on the road to success.

I had been coaching people for years and finally got around to attending a course and gaining a formal qualification shortly before leaving my HR career. I trained as an Executive Coach, but again, it was all about mindset.

It's your choice!

If you want to grow in your career you have a choice. If you want to climb the corporate ladder you have a choice. If you want the promotion, it's your choice. If you want to feel as though you'll never get to where you want to be, it's your choice.

I've tried to keep this book as short and concise as possible with short chapters that you can pick up when you are stuck or in need of a bit of reassurance, or you can read the entire book in one sitting.

I like to keep things as simple as possible, so I have tried to avoid jargon, complicated language, and data.

I like stories—they resonate with me more than any data ever will. Tell me percentages, facts, and figures and I tend to switch off, but tell me the story about how you got to those figures and I'm engaged.

Much of this book is from my own journey and my own experience—it's totally me and it's authentic. Throughout my HR career I have been faced with a lot of challenges, a lot of people issues to resolve, and a lot of opportunities to help people develop in their careers. What I have seen that separates the most successful from the "crowd" is their mindset and their belief in themselves, their own ability, their own skills, and their own ambition.

I would like to be able to say at this point that changing your mindset is a magical thing that happens instantly, and that you will wake up tomorrow and everything will be fixed, but I can't.

Any sort of change comes from practice and, in a lot of cases, hard work.

I know this stuff, I know it works, but I still have days where my Monkey Mind kicks in and I find myself in doubt, lacking confidence, and wondering what on earth I am doing.

More often than not I can stop myself before I get to this point by recognizing the signs and working harder at focusing on the right things, but I'm human. I'm not perfect—I don't even know if there is such a thing (and I say that as someone who always used to seek perfection in everything)—I'm only human.

I hope you get a lot from this book, and that you are able to take steps to implement real action into your life after reading it.

And when you're done, pass it on. Allow someone else to experience change and success—just by changing their mindset.

PART I

An Introduction to Mindset

How the Brain Works and Why We Think and Feel the Way We Do

Before we go into some of the specifics about mindset and how by changing your mindset you can foster a career for success, let's start with a bit more of the science behind some of this.

Let's start by understanding how the brain works. How we create feelings of doubt, fear, stress, anxiety, lack of confidence, and phobic responses that can hold us back from taking the next step in our career progression. How the interference comes and goes and what we can do about it to ensure we create a mindset for career success.

If we imagine our brain in the shape of a rugby ball, the very tip at the front of the ball is called the prefrontal cortex—this is the bit you know as you.

It is your conscious part. The part that interacts with the world. The part we are using to be aware of our interactions together. At the moment it is attached to a vast intellectual resource, the intellectual mind (the top part of the ball). This part we don't share with other animals.

Now, when we operate from the intellectual part of the brain we generally get things right in life. It will always come up with answers based on a proper assessment of the situation and is generally very positive.

There is another part of the brain. This part is the original, primitive part (the bottom of the ball). The central and influential part of this brain is the amygdala. This is generally referred to as the fight/flight/depression area of the brain and it is associated with two other very primitive parts.

The hippocampus, which holds all our primitive and sometimes inappropriate behavioral experiences and patterns, and the hypothalamus, which regulates chemical responses in the body and mind.

So, let us imagine that when you leave here today you run into a polar bear. What would happen?

Your anxiety would go up. You would lose intellectual control and move from the top part of the brain (the intellectual brain) to the bottom part of the brain (the primitive emotional brain), go "sweaty," increase the heartbeat, churn the stomach, and you would be off like a shot.

In the circumstances this response would be entirely appropriate and you would be pleased.

Unfortunately, it is the same in life. When our anxiety goes up, and it can be a gradual process, we lose intellectual control and to a greater or lesser extent the primitive mind takes over, and this mind always operates within the primitive parameters of depression, anxiety, and anger or a combination of all three.

If our primitive mind thinks that, for one reason or another, our life is in some sort of crisis or emergency, it will step in generally to help.

Depression, anxiety, and anger are all primitive opt-out clauses.

When the caveman looked out of the cave and there was snow or ice or danger and he couldn't go out to hunt, he pulled the rug over his head and didn't act until the situation changed. We have adapted this to all the modern-day symptoms of depression, anxiety, stress, and so on.

If we were in the jungle in those days I doubt very much if we would be too far away from our panic button at any given time.

And anger is merely a primitive way of increasing our strength to defend ourselves against wild animals and other wild tribesman, and in many cases it is this increase in anxiety that creates our thoughts of fear, stress, self-doubt, or phobias.

But there is more.

The primitive mind is a negative mind. It will always see things from the worst possible perspective. If you think about it, it has to—for your self-preservation. When you run into the polar bear the primitive mind won't say, "Ah! It has probably eaten." No; quite rightly it will say, "It will snaffle you."

This response is great when we run into polar bears but not so good when the bank statement arrives or we are facing redundancy, or you are going for a promotion or we've had an argument, and so on.

It is an obsessional mind. If you did have a polar bear in the back garden you would be reminded of it constantly. You would keep checking.

It is a vigilant mind. If the perception is that danger is all around, then, it is wise to stay on red alert.

And, because the primitive brain is not an intellect, it can't be innovative. It has to refer to previous patterns of behavior. If what we did yesterday ensured our survival, then, we are encouraged to do it again.

So how do we create this anxiety that causes us to move from the intellectual, sensible part of the brain to the angry, anxious, and depressed part?

Well, anxiety is caused by negative thinking.

It is not the events in one's lives that necessarily cause the perception of crisis. No; if that were so, everyone at university would be suffering from panic attacks and we know that is not the case. So it must be our thought patterns surrounding the events of our life.

(We will touch on this more later in our case study about Jen and Sally toward the end of the book.)

Every negative thought we have is converted into anxiety. We can create anxiety by negatively forecasting the future, big things; "we will never be able to afford that," "I'll never find another girlfriend," "I'll never have a baby," and so on. It can be small things; that meeting.

Here we should remember that the mind can't tell the difference between imagination and reality.

Intellectually, you know the meeting is going to go OK; they generally do, but being you, you start thinking about things going wrong.

You think about it 50 times?

The actual meeting goes quite well, but you have attended 51 meetings and 50 have been disasters.

We can negatively introspect about the past.

Now, within the primitive mind there's a library of all the patterns of thought and patterns of behavior that help us to survive.

Some of them are instinctive, but a baby doesn't know where it's going to be born—the Antarctic, or the jungle, for example.

So it needs to be able to learn automatic patterns of thought and behavior based on its environment.

So a three-year-old primitive man faced with a bear for the first time has to be able to learn that that bear isn't a nice and big fluffy to play with; it has to learn that that bear is going to eat the three-year-old primitive man unless it gets the hell out of there.

And it learns that because mum is screaming, "BEAR!!" The three-year-old primitive man picks up the stress from mum, focuses on the bear, and forms that pattern in the primitive mind that says "bears are dangerous."

So the next time he's out in the forest he's keeping a lookout for bears. If he spots one, the primitive mind refers to the pattern that says bears are dangerous and gets him the hell out of there with the fight-or-flight response.

This releases adrenaline and cortisol into the bloodstream, which increases heart rate and breathing rate and blood pressure to get oxygen to his muscles that enable him to escape as quickly as possible.

But sometimes the subconscious gets it wrong.

You can imagine Daisy, aged one, playing with a spider on the carpet when mum walks in—who's always been terrified of spiders. Mum screams because Daisy's eating the damn thing by this stage and Daisy forms that pattern that says "spiders are dangerous." Meanwhile during these potentially dangerous situations, the logical rational mind gets blocked out.

Partly because the subconscious is trying to protect those patterns that it thinks are important for survival, and partly because logic is just too slow. If you meet a bear the last thing you want is to rationally analyze what kind of a bear it is, whether it's dangerous, whether it's hungry, or whether you should freeze or run like hell.

This is why, while Daisy, 20 years down the line, logically and rationally knows that spiders aren't dangerous in this country—that doesn't stop her primitive mind not letting her in the same room as a spider.

So here's this distinction between what she logically and rationally knows to be the case and the behavior that the subconscious drives.

Now, every negative thought that we have is accumulated and stored. We say it is stored in a stress bucket.

Thankfully, we do have a method for emptying our bucket and it is known as REM sleep, rapid eye movement.

At night we re-run events of the day and change them from being an emotional memory to a narrative memory. A memory we have control over.

You are familiar with how REM works. Someone upsets you in the afternoon and you really are upset. You tell your partner and they say forget about it but you really can't. You are thinking about it when you go to bed.

During your REM sleep you will re-run the event either in clear or metaphorically (dreaming), and you will move it from the primitive brain to the intellectual brain where you have control over it.

So when you awaken in the morning you might well have forgotten about the wretched person, or you might not, but you will certainly be saying something like "How do I allow these people to upset me so?"

I fondly imagine that I awaken each morning with my bucket emptied so I can start the day without anxiety, anger, depression, or fear.

You don't. Why?

Well, here, depending on whether you have too much or too little REM sleep, there are two scenarios.

Scenario 1

Well, for a start you have been piling too much into your bucket. (Sometimes it will overflow!) Sadly, for one reason or another, REM is restricted to about 20 percent of our sleep patterns.

If you try and overdo that then the mind will wake you up. You know when it is your mind waking you up because you wake up wide awake and often feel quite miserable.

Often we can't get back to sleep again. You know the difference between that and the baby waking you up, for instance.

Now we are in the grip of a bit of a vicious circle. The more you have in your bucket, the more time you will spend in your primitive brain and the more you will be encouraged to be negative.

So, to get you back on top of things you need to restrict the amount you are piling into your bucket and get you concentrating on the positive things in your life.

You will know when you are doing this when you start sleeping better.

Scenario 2

You are still piling too much into your bucket and it takes a great deal of effort to attempt to empty it.

Sadly, REM is enervating. It uses enormous energy in the effort to diffuse that anxiety.

Sometimes we can overdo it and this exhausts us and makes us even more low, anxious, or fearful.

Now we find ourselves in the grip of a vicious circle again.

In an attempt to empty our bucket in this scenario, we are encouraged to sleep more and more, sometimes all day, which makes our depression, anxiety, stress, or fear worse and worse.

So again you need to restrict the amount you are piling into your bucket and get you concentrating on the positive aspects in your life.

You need to reorganize your sleep patterns too.

In the download section on my website, you will find an audio for relaxation.

You can use this once a day for the next few weeks, or as long as you like, perhaps just when needed, to help improve your sleep, increase your REM, and get you operating more effectively from the rational and logical part of your brain when fearful or stressful situations occur.

I just want to tell you about the physiology before we move on, about what happens in the brain when we suffer from anxiety disorders, depression, and fear.

Early man men and early woman were given quite definite rewards for carrying out certain evolutionary processes.

They got a reward when they hunted and gathered and successfully supported themselves and their families.

We are better as a tribe rather than as individuals, and they got rewarded when they interacted with others.

The reward they got they quite definitely recognized and scientists are adamant about this.

They felt motivated.

But most of all it was a coping mechanism; it helped them cope with day-to-day activities . . . helped them cope better with physical fear . . . made them braver; it even helped them cope with physical pain.

No doubt they were pleased.

Now we know what that reward is.

It's a chemical response in the brain that produces various neurotransmitters that act as catalysts for that sort of mentally healthy behavior.

And you know, the neurotransmitter we talk about most, simply because it is the most important, is serotonin, the happy hormone.

When we produce a constant flow of serotonin we are nice, happy, coping, brave little souls!

An Autobiography in Five Chapters

Chapter 1

I walk down the street. There is a deep hole in the pavement. I fall in. I am lost . . . I am helpless. It isn't my fault. It takes forever to find how to get out.

Chapter 2

I walk down the same street. There is a deep hole in the pavement. I look the other way. I fall in again. I can't believe I'm in the same place. I am lost . . . I am helpless. But it's not my fault. It still takes a long time to find how to get out.

Chapter 3

I walk down the same street. There is a deep hole in the pavement. I see it's there. I fall in . . . it's such a habit . . . but my eyes are open. I know where I am. It's my fault. I know how to get out.

Chapter 4

I walk down the same street. There is a deep hole in the pavement. I walk around it.

Chapter 5

I walk down a different street.
Anonymous

So we need to operate within these positive parameters like early man men and although we do not have to go out to hunt, we do have to interact in a positive way, be active in a positive way, and think in a positive way (the 3 Ps).

Because when we do, we produce patterns in the brain that give us that constant flow of serotonin.

Take some time now to consider patterns and behaviors or events that create a negative and physical reaction in you.

Are they logical or rational?

Mindset

What Is Mindset?

mindset

/'mʌɪn(d)sɛt/

noun

1. The established set of attitudes held by someone.

    A positive mindset is vital in order for us to achieve success, whether we run our own businesses, have a job or are on the ladder, or whether we choose to be a stay-at-home parent, take a career break or volunteer, mindset is what will help us shine and succeed.

Why?

Let's start by taking a look at the two defined categories of mindset, fixed and growth (see figure 1.1).

For many of us, we sit in the growth mindset category; if you think about it, we have to—in order to realize our dreams and achieve our vision. If we are set in a fixed mindset we won't be open to new opportunities, learning new skills, and trying new things and without this we are unlikely to get to the level of success that we desire.

When I started my first business, I spoke to many people and heard many stories, both good and bad, about what running a business was actually like. I was told that as a business owner I would spend at least 80 percent of my time running the business instead of doing the work I actually wanted to do.

What Kind of Mindset Do You Have?

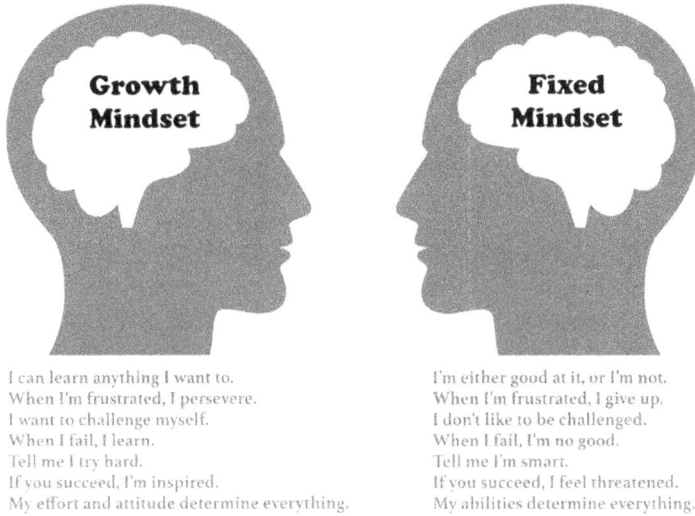

Growth Mindset

Fixed Mindset

I can learn anything I want to.
When I'm frustrated, I persevere.
I want to challenge myself.
When I fail, I learn.
Tell me I try hard.
If you succeed, I'm inspired.
My effort and attitude determine everything.

I'm either good at it, or I'm not.
When I'm frustrated, I give up.
I don't like to be challenged.
When I fail, I'm no good.
Tell me I'm smart.
If you succeed, I feel threatened.
My abilities determine everything.

Figure 1.1 What kind of mindset do you have?

At the time I thought this was ridiculous; in reality it turned out to be true. My expertise was people development and coaching. I knew little about finance, marketing, social media, spreadsheets, networking, blogging, writing, IT, and so on.

I had always worked for companies where we had specific departments or members of my team to deal with many of these tasks and there I was, just me and my laptop starting a business and having to learn how to do everything that needed doing.

At the time of starting my business, I had left my well-paid job in London with no savings and no backup plan. I learned things the hard way and on occasions, probably many occasions, have gotten things wrong. I have wasted time, money, and effort trying to learn; some things I have developed well and others not so much.

If I had done the sensible thing and saved enough money to get me started, identified where I needed support from day one, and found the right people in the first place this would have helped enormously.

If I had a fixed mindset, however, and no savings and no backup, it is extremely likely that I would be back working in full-time employment and not doing what I am doing now.

I remember working from home one day, only a couple of months into my new venture, and my laptop and printer died. Historically I would have called the IT department, but I no longer had an IT department to call.

I did the usual technical thing and turned them both off and on again, unplugged them, left them for a minute, two, five, ten, and still nothing. On this day I felt alone for the first time. I felt alone, isolated, and like a complete failure. Who was I to think I knew what I was doing? How dare I think I was capable enough of running a successful business? Time to start job hunting. I was actually contemplating giving it all up because of a laptop and a printer; in reality, I couldn't look for a job as of course my laptop wasn't working. So I did the next best thing. I went for a walk.

I love being outside, I always feel so much better, and it helps me clear my head, gives me proper time to think, and calms me down.

During my walk I talked myself round, remembered I had a business card of an IT consultant, and told myself I was not a failure, I would not be getting a job because this was now my job, success was the only way forward, and it was time to call my coach.

I got home, called the IT consultancy, who were amazing and had me up and running in 30 minutes, and then contacted my coach to say I needed some sessions. She lives in California and I am based in the UK so I didn't expect an instant response, but I got one. I started my sessions and in one month I was doing things I never thought I would and had a newfound level of confidence. I had also doubled my prices and was making money. I was in business.

Mindset can be a tricky thing to manage. When we find ourselves feeling stressed or anxious we move to the primitive part of our brain, our flight-or-fight response kicks in, and we can quickly find ourselves in the space of negative self-talk.

To keep us energized, uplifted, and happy, we need to think positively, act positively, and interact positively—I call these the 3 Ps and they work, as long as you are in the right mindset and the right frame of mind.

My 5 Top Tips for a Positive Mindset

- Be clear on your vision and do all you can to stay focused.
- Surround yourself with energy angels—People and tasks that fill you with energy.

- Limit the time you spend with energy vampires—People and tasks that drain you of energy. Ideally you want a ratio of 3:1, angels to vampires.
- Take time out to relax and switch off.
- Focus on the 3 P's—Positive Actions, Positive Interactions, and Positive Thoughts

The Masculine and the Feminine Mindset

The world of business is changing, the world is changing, and if you tap into what all of the spiritualists and many business leaders are telling us, we are moving into the age of the feminine.

I include this thinking in the book, because I believe we need a blend of both masculine and feminine thinking, planning, and execution in order to live a balanced life, be happy in our work, and run successful businesses.

The Athena Doctrine provides a lot of in-depth research and thinking demonstrating that businesses and leaders need to be more feminine in order for businesses to succeed (I will leave you to make up your own mind on that).

What I know is that men started many big companies with billions of pounds of income each year many years ago. I know that when people try to railroad me or bully me, or undermine me at work, men or women, I do not take kindly to this. And I also know that those of us that work with people, (and know we have a way to help people in some way), often struggle to put a price on what we do and can struggle to build a business.

So, below you will find a table outlining the "traits" of the masculine and feminine and I know I have a blend of the two. I'm not going to go into too much detail on this as you will know the traits you have in order to live the life you want and the business you desire and the areas you may need to develop if your career, your business, and your dreams are to succeed.

For example, I am very imaginative and creative, but if all I do is imagine and create without a plan or an outcome in mind, how will I generate income? I do work I truly love, but I have to keep reality-checking to make sure I am on the right path, even though I live my life largely by intuition.

Feminine	Masculine
Heart	Mind
Feeling	Thinking
Passive	Active
Stillness and resting	Being in the world
Receptive	Directive
Imagination	Reason
Creativity	Logical and linear thinking
Formlessness	Structure
Intuition and the unknown	Logic and certainty
Innocence "in no sense"	Must "make sense"
Nurturing	Orientating
What you truly love	What you think you need
Living for joy	Living to survive
Vision	Reality
Just being is valid	Must achieve to be valid
Beauty	Will
Soft	Hard
Internal	External
Attraction	Assertion
Collective	Individual
Flexible	Rigid
Flow	Go
Process	Outcome

Top Tips

- Understand what it takes to make your career a success.
- Know where you need to adapt and grow—Take steps to make it happen.
- Identify where you need help—and then get it.

9 Signs It's Time to Change Your Mindset

Believing in negative thoughts is the single greatest obstruction to happiness and success. Your perspective on life comes from the inner emotional beliefs.

Some of us walk through life feeling optimistic, taking things in our stride, and getting on with whatever we need to. For others, we see the negative side of life, feeling that life is unfair and everyone is out to get us, not noticing the good things in life or being grateful for what we have because everyone else has better.

In this part of the book, I will share with you 9 signs that it's time to change your mindset, and if you discover that you need to make a change, when you do, your life will change almost in an instant.

Here are some clear signs it's time to change your mindset:

1. You see nothing but negatives.

   If you were determined to get joy out of the present moment, you would learn to focus on the positive. What it takes is not paying attention to negative thoughts—yours or anyone else's. Disregarding negative thoughts isn't about burying your head in the sand; it's the focused act of not allowing negativity to fog your vision and dominate your experience of the present.

   This moment is never enhanced or helped in any way by negativity, even though we as human beings are programed to think our negative thoughts, worries, and fears serve some beneficial function. When we deeply examine a negative thought we see that negativity doesn't serve any benefit. Focusing on negativity doesn't make anyone a better person, nor does doing so help us make any bit of progress. In fact, the truth is quite the opposite.

2. You are relentlessly resisting the truth.

   Watch your inner self-talk, the voice you have in your head that holds you back or pushes you forward. See if you can catch yourself consciously or subconsciously complaining about your present life situation, what other people have said or done, your past, your surroundings, or even the weather. To complain is always nonacceptance of reality. It invariably carries with it a tremendous amount of negativity and stress.

   When you complain, you transform yourself into a victim. When you proactively take positive action, on the other hand, you are in power. So if something is truly bothering you, change your situation by taking action, or consciously let it go—leave the situation or accept it. All else is foolishness.

Remind yourself, again and again if you must, when something cannot be changed you must change your attitude about it. After you have done what you can do, happiness is allowing yourself to be perfectly OK with "what is," rather than wishing for and worrying about "what is not." "What is" is what's supposed to be, or it would not be. The rest is just you, arguing with life.

3. You have a tendency to blame others.

Letting go gives us emotional freedom, and emotional freedom is the only condition for happiness. If, in your heart, you still cling to anything—anger, resentment, jealously, and so on—you cannot be free. And doing so doesn't change the heart of other people—it only changes yours. Know this.

Put down the sword and stop attacking others in your head. The strong person is not the best fighter. Rather, the strong person is the one who controls herself when she is angry, and grows from it.

4. You are passionately worried about everything.

Worrying does nothing but steal your joy and keep you busy doing nothing. It's like using your imagination to create things you don't want. You need to stop getting yourself into situations in your head where all your options are potentially bad.

Remember, it's not what you look at that matters, it's what you see. There are always two ways to address your present situation. Each way is like a brick, which can be used as a stepping stone, or which can be picked up in a worried frenzy and used to shatter your window of hope and happiness.

The bottom line is that everything on the outside doesn't need to be perfect or make sense right now. In your mind you can go anywhere you imagine. And where your mind consistently goes, the rest of your life will gradually follow.

5. Your expectations are stressing you out.

Drop the needless expectations. Appreciate "what is" for a moment. It doesn't matter if your glass is half empty or half full. Just be thankful that you have a glass and that there's something in it. Choosing to be positive and having an appreciative attitude influences everything you do. The magnitude of your happiness and success will be directly proportional to the magnitude of your thoughts and how you choose to think about things.

Nothing ever works out exactly the way you want it to. Hope for the best, but expect less. Don't let what you expected to happen blind you from the goodness happening all around. Even if it doesn't work out at all, it's still worth it if it made you feel something new, and if it taught you something new.

6. You secretly want a pain-free life.
Pain is part of being human, but it's vitally important. It strengthens the mind, heart, and body. You can't grow strong, brave, or successful in this world if you've only had good things happen to you within the safe boundaries of your own little comfort bubble. You need real-life experiences, and nothing ever becomes real until you experience it first-hand.

Honestly, life is very much like a game of chess. To win you have to make a move, even when it's tough and things before didn't go exactly as planned. Knowing which move to make comes with insight and knowledge, by learning the unexpected and often painful lessons that are accumulated along the way.

7. You're never satisfied with what you have.
Our stress and frustration are far greater when we have more than enough but want even more, than when we have almost nothing and want some. In other words, as human beings we are less dissatisfied when we lack many things than when we endlessly seem to lack but one continuously changing thing.

Details aside, the key is to want less and appreciate more.

A lot of people get so hung up on what they can't have that they don't think for a second about whether they really want it. Ask yourself: "Are these things truly better than the things I already have? Or am I just conditioned to be unhappy with what I have?"

In the end, happiness is an attitude of gratitude we act upon daily. We either make the best of the present or the worst of it. We either make ourselves miserable or happier and stronger. The amount of effort is the same.

8. It's been a while since you learned something new.

   The best remedy for being sad or feeling stuck is learning something new. That's the only thing that never fails—simply making progress and knowing it.

   Your body may grow old and frail, you may lie awake some nights listening to your past regrets, you may miss your only love, or you may know your respect has been trampled on by unfriendly faces. There is only one thing for healing that works every time—to learn. Learn why the world around you zigs and zags and what fuels it. Learn what excites you and learn more about it. That's the only positive effort that a battered mind can never exhaust, never alienate, never be tortured by, never fear or doubt, and never dream of regretting.

   Learning is healing. Just look at all the things there are to learn, and get started.

9. You catch yourself living in the past.

   Nostalgia is a good and necessary state of mind, sometimes. It's a way for all of us to find lessons in every life experience, and peace in all that we have accomplished, or even failed to accomplish. At the same time, though, if nostalgia precipitates intentions and actions to return to that fabled, rosy-painted past time, particularly in someone who believes her present life to be inadequate, then it's an empty state of mind, doomed to produce nothing more than frustration and an even greater sense of unhappiness.

   Don't let the past steal your present. Your past has not defined, deterred, or defeated you. It has only strengthened who you are today. Keep this in mind and press onward.

Afterthoughts

An effective mindset is one that makes the best use of available resources— your time, energy, and efforts—and uses them to create positive change. It's not about trying to do everything and be everything; it's making the very best of what you have while enjoying the process of living.

Your mindset is the underpinning and cornerstone for everything that happens in your life. It's a collection of all your beliefs, behaviors, feelings, emotions, and attitudes.

As you work to adjust your mindset, here's what you can expect from striking the right balance:

- A sense of firm faith, certainty, and purpose
- Consistent drive, focus, and commitment to meaningful pursuits
- Clear insight into present obstacles and opportunities
- A feeling of peace and joy from making progress daily

Your Turn . . .

What state of mind have you been in lately? What changes would you like to make to your mindset and why?

6 Ways to Change Your Mindset

When you have identified that something needs to change, maybe one of the 9 things discussed earlier in this chapter or perhaps something else, it's time to start taking steps to change your mindset.

Here are 6 ways to change your mindset (more tips, tools, and techniques are included in Part 3 of this book).

1. Get the best information only

   Try to find the very best information in your field. Then focus on learning this information only. I personally learned that in any worthwhile field there is more information available than needed, especially on the Internet. You have to narrow down the information input to the most effective. I personally believe that one of the critical personal skills today is not to find information, but to select the best information and avoid the rest.

   The Good: Reading great books/information products and some great blogs. Everything else is a waste of time.

   The Bad: Mostly not worth it are forums, getting books/information products without researching the field, 90 percent of blogs. From my personal experience, those are usually things that support procrastination and information overload. The reason is that only a tiny fraction of the information out there is taking you really forward. You have to develop the skill of identifying this kind of information. We are talking about the right mindset here; part of it is not to get sucked into the mediocre area. You want to align yourself with the best out there.

2. Role-model the best people

Similar to #1, look for the best people in your field and try to model what they did right. Adopt their kind of thinking and mindset. Follow them. Of course, keep and only add what you think is right for you. That way you can actually improve and personalize their mindset to fit perfectly for you. It's never copying; it's taking what works for you by getting inspiration and quality input.

Now I realize that you can't look into the minds of the best people in your field. But you can get plenty of information about how they are thinking, their advice, what they did. For instance, if you are an entrepreneur or are self-employed.

I have many role models, but it's important to remember here to remain *you*. Your role models may have tendencies, behaviors, habits, skills, or knowledge that you want to model, but you should stay true to yourself, and remain yourself.

Be you, everyone else is taken.

3. Examine your current beliefs

Examine your mindset by looking at your current belief system. Are these beliefs supporting you? Or are they self-limiting beliefs?

I attended a talk a couple of years ago and the speaker confidently opened his talk by saying that there is no such thing as self-limiting beliefs, only beliefs. At the time I thought he was mad, but on reflection, he was right. Beliefs are what we have; we only realize they are self-limiting when we unlock our true potential.

You have to identify those possible blocks and turn them around. Because, whether you know about limiting beliefs or not, they are working in your subconscious mind.

To uncover your beliefs, ask yourself the right questions about where you want to go and what is standing in your way right now. The key then is to turn those beliefs around by declaring supportive statements on the same belief. To internalize these new supportive beliefs you can make use of affirmations or chants.

4. Shape your mindset with vision and goals

A proactive approach to building your mindset is to clearly see where you want to go. Seeing a vision, images describing your end result clearly in your mind's eye, will create a strong pull toward this end result. Then go on and break your vision into goals. It will shape your mindset to conform to your vision.

Learn and adapt from your own experience and always try to look deeper for the real reasons why you get the results you are getting.

5. Find your voice

One of the most beautiful things is when you find your very own way, something that you could call finding your voice.

To help you find this, answer these 4 questions.

1. What are you good at? That's your mind.
2. What do you love doing? That's your heart.
3. What need can you serve? That's the body.
4. And finally, what is life asking of you? What gives your life meaning and purpose? What do you feel like you should be doing? In short, what is your conscience directing you to do? That is your spirit.

Your voice is what you express 100 percent authentically; it is the unique thing that you can add to the world, because you are who you are. Looking to find what is really you and being critical about every input you get should be part of your mindset. Stay open and flexible in your mind. Don't judge too soon. It gives you something unique and helps you to build integrity.

6. Protect your mindset

One thing you have to do is to protect your mindset against the naysayers and people who want to drag you down. You also have to protect it against bad information and against overload (see #1). Keeping your confidence is a big thing.

So please stay on the right path and look to improve yourself and to help others along the way. You can't go wrong with that.

Don't let failure be an ending; Make it the Beginning!

PART II

At Work Mindset

Mindset and Purpose

I toyed with covering a number of topics, such as "shiny object syndrome," "am I enough?" and then decided they are linked to one thing, Purpose.

When we know our purpose and are truly living it through our values, our actions, our language, and our behaviors, we are able to stay on track, stay focused, and do all we can to achieve it.

When we are unclear of our purpose we, in a sense, lose a part of our identity and we start to exist instead of truly living.

My purpose, as I've mentioned, is about helping people grow and create change in their lives. I'm very clear on this, I'm passionate about it, and it's what gets me out of bed in the mornings. "How" I do this is somewhat irrelevant; as long as I'm doing it I'm happy.

I have a number of businesses, my consultancy supporting companies, my coaching practice supporting HR professionals, and my membership platform supporting coaches, consultants, and expert-preneurs. All three help people grow.

I've been through times, though, when I have doubted my purpose, or felt myself going off track, and it is at these times that I get sucked into the "shiny object syndrome" or wonder if I'm good enough and I feel like I lose my way. All of a sudden, anything that anyone else is doing, or creating, or saying, I feel like I should be doing the same thing. "That's it, that's my thing, that's what I'm meant to be doing," and I can spiral off for hours or sometimes days, until I bring myself back to my purpose and why I do what I do, and I feel stable again.

Many people will, I'm sure, have their way of helping you find your purpose. They may ask you to consider something from your childhood, the values of a particular brand, the one thing that irritates you the most when it's lacking or energizes you when it's present, it's your mission statement, noble cause, value statement. All of these are valid and I have worked with people who use these techniques, and they have worked. I've also used some of these to help my own clients and incorporated some of these into courses and programs to help people move forward.

The "thing" I use the most to help myself and my clients is just three words: "Who am I?" or, if asking someone else, "Who are you?." The more you ask, the deeper you go and the deeper you go the more powerful the answer and the more powerful the answer the stronger the reaction, and then you find it, that nugget, the golden nugget of wisdom, where you see the lights turn on, the gut feel that says "Oh my god, that's it!," the feeling in the pit of your stomach that helps you find, redefine, or rediscover your purpose. Just from those three little words. And usually, it's the core part of how you are, something you are already doing, but maybe not realizing it.

I know we get told to start with why. Simon Sinek, great as he is, seems to have made it compulsory for people to start with why and the purpose in order to be successful. Yet I know a lot of people who don't know their way, they haven't uncovered their nugget, and they are still successful, they are still happy, they are still making a difference, and they are still moving forward.

I find that, when I'm working to my true purpose, I'm authentic and passionate in my actions, my language, my interactions, and behaviors. I don't have to pretend to be something I'm not, I don't try to please people, I don't have to get them to buy my products or work with me— everything just falls into place and it does so easily. When I'm off my path and everything is becoming a chore, I know I'm heading in the wrong direction and off the path I'm meant to be on.

It's built into us that life has to be hard, that we have to work hard and play harder to enjoy life, but I don't believe that's true. On the right path, yes, and there will of course be times when we have to work harder, push harder to get where we need to be, we need to put some effort in, but life isn't hard, or at least it doesn't have to be. When we attract the right job, the right partner, the right friends, the right clients, the right coach or mentor, the right team, it just becomes easier.

On my radio show a year or so ago, I interviewed an amazing woman called Karolina who works with women on body transformation. What makes her different to many other personal trainers is that she focuses on mindset before anything else to really get to the root cause of the problem that is stopping women from being who they really are, and how they should really feel in the first place. She looks stunning, is a beautiful person inside and out, and lives with authenticity in all areas of her life.

She studied chemistry at university in Poland, where she was born, and was a self-confessed geek, but realized that science wasn't for her. She was at her happiest when she was outside, exercising, focusing positively in nature, moving her body, and challenging her mind. She went on to compete in bodybuilding competitions but gave up when it all became too regimented and no longer fun.

She realized that her purpose was to be helping others transform their bodies and enjoy exercise, instead of being sat in a science lab all day.

As children, we dream of achieving the life we want as we get older, an astronaut, a pilot, a singer, a dancer, a ballerina, a teacher, a nurse, a .... (*you* fill in the blank), but as we get older, our teachers, our parents, or other adults in our lives tell us we need to grow up and get a "proper" job, and so we start searching for our "proper" job and sometimes only to please others. Speaking to career advisers as teenagers—when we don't even know what we are doing with our friends that day after school, let alone what we want to do for the rest of our lives—can be a difficult process, and teenagers often feel that they are being pushed down a route too early, and as we progress down the "proper job" route we can start to lose passion. We focus on a job to pay the bills or on seeking a career that will help us do the work we love, or help us buy the house of our dreams, or buy the car we always wanted, because we get told that singers, artists, and dancers have it tough and that not everyone will be one because it's too hard and that astronauts are few and far between.

My younger brother always wanted to build LEGO for a living, and his teachers told him that we couldn't all live in a fairy tale and getting that job would be too difficult as they don't take on many people each year. At 34, he loves music, but hasn't really found his purpose. He wants to build a school abroad and complete the legacy of one of his teachers, but has never taken any steps to make this happen and I fear until he does, he will feel unfulfilled and existing, albeit he exists in Ibiza in the sun and with a very laid-back way of life, but off purpose.

When we ignore our "purpose" or stray from the right path, life is hard, and it's hard because we are battling against something we shouldn't really be doing. On the right path life is good.

Another way I find quite useful in defining purpose is asking "if money were no object what would I be doing?" My answer is: coaching and developing people over Skype while sitting on the veranda of my beach house.

Who are you?

What's your purpose?

When was the last time life was easy? And what made it so?

Mindset for Success

success

noun

The accomplishment of an aim or purpose.

Success can be a tricky thing to define. Success for me may be something completely different than it is for you, but when we are clear on what success means to us as individuals we know what we are aiming for and can take steps to get there.

Some of my clients feel "unsuccessful" in areas of their lives. Some feel unsuccessful because of what they see in others or what other people have.

One of the women I know had a successful business that she sold for millions of pounds and has now entered into the property game as a hobby. She has a wonderful house, has amazing holidays every year to exotic places, always looks stunning, and has a lot of friends. Yet she is divorced, has stilted relationships with her children, and rarely sees her grandchildren. If you talk to her she will tell you she is miserable. People on the outside looking in see her success and wish they had it too, but they do not see her struggles.

I know board members, CEOs, stay-at-home parents, business owners, and professionals who are, or who appear to be, successful, and yet they don't recognize this in themselves, and I also know people who recognize and appreciate each success they make as well as those that shout about how successful they are, when it isn't visible at all.

My belief is that, in order to be truly successful, you need to be clear on your purpose. My purpose, as I've said, is helping people grow. I've done this since childhood, throughout my career, with family and friends, and while I find it a bit difficult to let them go, I've given birth to two amazing sons who I know will succeed in whatever they choose to do and who make me proud every day of my life.

I know my purpose, and I see success every day in those around me, which, in turn, allows me to feel successful. I was successful in my career and I am successful in my businesses. Overall success for me, the defining moment, will come when I can work just a couple of days a week, from anywhere I like, while travelling, and then ultimately, spending time with my grandchildren (should I have them), and providing financial security for my sons and their families and financial freedom for myself.

Learn to celebrate your successes no matter how big or small. Sometimes we get so caught up in "busy" that even when we do succeed in something we are quickly moving onto the next thing to do. We need to learn to take time to recognize our achievements and our successes as this will help us know when we have reached success. It also gives us the reward that we need so much as it helps us produce those happy hormones that make us feel good. If we continue to push and push, not recognizing success and the things that make us feel a sense of achievement, reward, and happiness, this can add to stress, anxiety, and burnout.

I have worked in many businesses, and with many clients who work in businesses, where success is never celebrated. Projects, programs, and improvements are completed and without a moment's hesitation, the next thing has started. This has to change. Employees are no longer constantly expecting an annual bonus as their only form of recognition each year. Employees (and people in general), want to be recognized, thanked, appreciated, valued, and congratulated. Admittedly some people may want a pat on the back much more than others, but if that keeps spurring them on to do a good job, then thank them. If you are self-employed, running your own business, or an employee, and recognition and thanks relating to success are not given, find a way to have your own mini celebration, or treat yourself to that thing you have been longing for.

I have four ways of recognizing and celebrating my daily successes. For e-mails of thanks and appreciation, I store these in my "happy folder" in my e-mails and look back on them when I start to create new content and when I'm having a bit of a low day. At the end of every day I write on colored notes what I am grateful for that day and any successes I have achieved and place them in my gratitude jar. When I need some longer reflection I write in my journal and make notes of everything I have achieved and everything I am grateful for, as well as ask myself questions that I need to answer. And for business successes, I celebrate with my team, be it lunch, dinner, or drinks (nonalcoholic for me).

In addition to this, I may have a night out or a weekend away with my partner, a day out with the kids, or a meal with family and friends. And throughout every day, my partner and I high-five when something goes well (a silly but effective little ritual).

Success doesn't have to be a one-time thing. Think back over your life and all of your successes and achievements so far. School success, educational awards and certificates, sporting achievements, overcoming obstacles, becoming a parent, surviving a traumatic experience, recovering from illness, securing your ideal role, gaining promotions, having a work-life balance, marrying your ideal partner—the list is endless and, perhaps, the best is still yet to come.

Remember, your mindset is the established set of attitudes and beliefs that you hold. If you believe in success, you will have success; if you only believe in failure, take it as your First Attempt In Learning and keep going.

Tips for Success

- Your success will be personal to you; don't compare it with anyone else.
- Your definition of success is likely to change as you go through life.
- If you believe in success you will be successful.

The Employee Mindset

Getting into the world of work during or after education can be scary and tough, but it also fills you with an enormous sense of pride and even more so when you receive your first pay packet.

As time goes on, your value at work increases and so does your salary (hopefully), and you continue to work hard, doing what it takes to succeed in the job. Your performance reviews and any bonuses that you receive are a great way of telling you what you are worth and what a great job you have done (although there is more to work and life than money), and as long as you stay in love with your job, your manager (in a professional sense only), and your company, life is good.

The security of your monthly paycheck, the stability of the job, and the extended family you create are many things that people hold on to; even when things are tough or we begin to fall out of love with the work, the people and the security can keep us going.

Now throughout my career it was instilled in me that we should enjoy the work we do. We spend more than half our lives at work and with the people we work with, and we should enjoy it. Yet I see SO many memes every Monday from people who hate Mondays and don't want to be at work. Literally every Monday dozens of these from friends, acquaintances, contacts, and businesses flood my social media feeds.

The biggest exception, and I am sure they stole my catchphrase, was Reed, the recruitment company, with their campaign "We love Mondays." And quite right too, what is there not to love about Monday? You are doing the work you love, with people you like, to pay you for the life you have and the lifestyle you want, right?

You chose to do the work you are doing, right? At the company you work at?

The stats change, but over the years it has been in and around the 80-percent mark of people who leave a business because they are actually leaving their managers, not the work or the company. That's a staggeringly high figure and what's even more scary is that over the last 10 years, as businesses have had to tighten their financial belts and make cutbacks, managers are given increased responsibility but not always the support, training, and development to help them succeed in the role, and they are increasingly expected to do more for less.

It is also reported that between 70 and 80 percent of workers have some kind of stress- or anxiety-related illness due to work pressure at some point in their career.

I made the decision not to go to university (although I now have three degrees and am doing my PhD); instead, after my higher education I started working for a national retailer as one of their management trainees. I loved it. Two years on the shop floor and I was then a manager and then I began to specialize in Human Resources and Employee Development.

I learned valuable management and leadership skills from my senior managers and mentors, made a few mistakes along the way, but loved the work I was doing, the people I was working with, the variety of work, and, of course, my salary, bonus, and staff discount—this was the best job in the world.

And then came the changes. They started to strip out a tier of managers, the tier I was just promoted into but was waiting for a vacancy to become available. I was told it would be six years at least before I moved into the more senior position. The thought of waiting six years was not something I was prepared to do and I started to look for other jobs. Two were disasters, and in every possible sense—the managers, the work, and the business—and I quickly moved on.

I found myself my perfect job and within an eight-year period I had gained seven promotions, quadrupled my salary, improved my quality of life, and had financial security like I had never had in my life. I was the main breadwinner in the house, was out of the house on my commute and at work for a minimum of 12 hours a day, but we had money, a nice car, a nice house, and great holidays. What more was there I needed!?

The sense of pride and achievement was great; I was really good at something. I was breaking down barriers of "glass ceilings," I had a great family life (at weekends), I was growing and supporting my teams, I was young, and I was successful. I was receiving feedback from colleagues and audience members at talks I was doing, telling me how inspirational I was—life was good.

I soon realized, though, it wasn't what I wanted. All of this hard work, all of the frustration, all of the challenges, all of the long hours, I didn't want it. I knew, though, I had to keep going, as "I couldn't afford to lose all that money."

As employees, whether we love or loathe our jobs, our attention is very much focused on the money aspect instead of the life aspect and this shouldn't be the case. We need money to pay our bills and live whatever lifestyle it is that we choose, but what amount of money is worth not seeing your children, becoming ill with stress, pushing for 12 or more hours a day (sometimes up to 18), and being exhausted?

I thought I had found my price with my six-figure salary, all of the benefits and bonuses and the "status" of my role, until one day I was on a training course and heard myself say for the first time ever, "I want my own company." Those five words changed my life.

You see for many (and I stereotype here, which is not my usual stance) "I hate Mondays" is the norm. Urgh, Monday! The week and indeed the employee mindset becomes the Monday-to-Friday dying syndrome and it seems to go a little like this:

- Sunday: "I cannot believe I have to go back to work tomorrow"—miserable all day and then can't sleep at night, waking the next day shattered.
- Monday: "Urgh, I hate Monday, work again, great (not!)"—lethargic and slow all day. One of your colleagues asks if you had a great weekend and you reply along the lines of "It was good, yes, thanks. Not long enough, though." "Yeah, I know what you mean!"
- Tuesday: "It's Tuesday already, I have so much to do this week"—procrastinates, reads through all e-mails; finds lots of interesting facts, information, and sales information for lots of shiny bright objects that can distract from work. (Tuesday is the best day for e-mail marketing campaigns.)
- Wednesday: "Thank God for that, only two days left"—brain kicks in and you realize you still have so much to do and you better get on with it and you work a few extra hours because there is just so much to do and you are slightly stressed out by it all, but it is slump day and you can't really be bothered.
- Thursday: "It's Friday tomorrow woohoo!!!"—you start asking everyone what they are doing at the weekend and look for inspiration for the weekend for yourself if you haven't already planned what you are going to be doing. Possibly even an after-work drink tonight in preparation for the fact that the weekend is nearly here.

- Friday: "YAY, it's finally here, the weekend is finally here!"—drinks after work and then straight home to get ready to go out properly.
- Saturday: "It's the weekend!"—time with kids, family, friends, shopping, and so on. You chill out, you relax, and then you realize that the next day is Sunday and the cycle starts again.

Where is the productivity? Where is the positivity? Where is the life? Where is the passion? What needs to change?

Now I'm certainly not saying that everyone is like this, but I'm sure you know some people in your company and perhaps many of your friends and family that are!

The world of work is changing and as the younger generations are coming in to the work environment thick and fast, they are paving the way for all generations to think about what they want and what they doing. When I was a child, you would typically hear of people having their midlife crisis, buying the Porsche, and running off with a new partner half the age of their current one. Because what they are seeking is change; their mindset is telling them that something needs to change and they're crying out for a dose of serotonin.

Now, we just seem to want to live on purpose; we want work that we are passionate about, that excites us, that makes a difference—work that is aligned to our values, our skills, and our motivation. And if we can align our thoughts, interactions, and behaviors to this as well, then we are well on the way to a successful and fulfilling career.

It is so easy for the mindset of an employee to be on constant countdown for the weekend, a bank holiday, or a vacation. I have a few friends that are teachers and they start each new term on countdown with how many weeks they have to work for; how inspiring is that for the kids? This half term in the UK, it's only four weeks until the next break and they are so pleased.

Top Tips

- You have chosen your career and your job—love Mondays, even if you have to fake it for a while.

- Find ways to reduce your workload and your stress—if you can't, try some Mindfulness, breathing techniques, or increase your exercise to release your happy hormones.
- Think back to why you chose your career/job in the first place—what did you say and do at your interview to prove you deserved the job? How passionate were you? Reignite that passion.
- If you have lost your passion—move on!

The Entrepreneur Mindset

I mentioned in the introduction some of the things I experienced when I started my business and you may find the same things apply to you.

If you are thinking of starting a business but are not quite ready to make the leap, ask yourself why.

If money is the one thing holding you back, a couple of questions for you:

- If you had all of the money in the world, what would you do?
- Where do you see yourself five years from now?

At the end of this book I have included a "perfect day" exercise to really get you thinking about the life you want. If you see yourself in a top-floor office of a large company with a big team, a fat salary, and a company car, then that's your dream.

If you see yourself running your business from any location you can dream of, making the money you want, and working the hours you want, then that is your answer.

Money was a factor for me; I said I would save for two years and then start. I quit in three months because the desire to do what I am doing now was too strong. I had a three-month cushion and I knew I had to make it work. For the first time in my life I had no Plan B.

Many entrepreneurs feel the same, and even if your first, second, or third business doesn't work out, you keep at it, working whatever hours you need to make it work because you know this is where you are meant to be and what you are meant to be doing.

In the UK we have a show called *Dragons' Den* where people pitch for investment for their business. I have lost track of the people that have been on the show and the chance of investment is their last hope as they have invested and lost life savings, properties, and financial investments, yet still they do not give up on their dream.

If you know much about Richard Branson you will know that he was close to bankruptcy and nearly lost it all, only managing to save the business with literally hours left to go, and he did it. And he did it because he believed he would and he believed in his business.

For an entrepreneur money is, of course, important, but it's not the be-all and end-all—although the quicker you get to financial security and freedom, the better, of course.

But, when you're an entrepreneur, it's more than that. It's about finding and living your purpose, your calling, the work you know you should be doing, the idea you can't shake, the product you believe in, and the difference you know you can make.

It's tough; sometimes you will work for much less than minimum wage, sometimes you won't sleep, sometimes you will wonder how you are going to pay the bills, but when it comes together, you have the life you want, the life you dream of, and you will be happy.

It's important, though, that you know whether you have a fixed mindset or a growth mindset and what to change to get you to the point of a growth mindset. Without this, unfortunately, you are likely to fall into the category of one of the businesses that fails within the first two years or you will be back in the rat race picking up your monthly paycheck again.

When you're an entrepreneur there is rarely a Plan B; just your plan and you will make it work no matter what. Of course you may find yourself on Plan Z by the time you actually get finished, but you have to believe in your Plan A.

Throughout my "career," I always had a Plan B; if this job didn't work out I would just find another, simple.

As an entrepreneur that is not so much the case. Don't get me wrong but there have been times where I have felt like giving up, felt like going back to my nice six-figure salary and living the easy life, but in reality, even looking for jobs has made me feel queasy; even when my bank balance hasn't been as healthy as I want it to be, the thought of going back into work, now that I'm out of it, is not at all appealing, and I do think I have made myself totally unemployable. Of course if push came to shove, I would go back into work, and I would manage my mindset accordingly.

As a new entrepreneur pricing yourself, your time, and your products can be tricky. "How much am I worth?" can be a difficult thing to answer. I increased my prices three times in the first year and only the third time did I gain more clients.

If you are too cheap, people won't buy or those that do will only be low-figure clients; too high and you could price yourself out of the market especially while nobody really knows you. Test your market but don't get sucked in.

Time is NOT money! The outcomes you provide or the difference your product makes are where you find the value, not the hourly rate you work or how much time it takes to produce something. Think value, not hours—shift your mindset.

Avoid bright-shiny-object syndrome and comparison syndrome. Both come into play when things aren't going your way or you start to doubt yourself or money is running out.

Comparison syndrome is where you sit comparing yourself to others and wishing you had what they have. You know what I mean; the coaches that plaster everywhere about their six-figure months; the start-ups that made a million in their first year; the glamorous lives, houses, and cars of those who splash it everywhere and then tell you they can help you too. STOP. Look at yourself, your market, and your clients. Get a plan, think big, stay positive, be grateful for what you have, and enjoy life. It's all about perception.

Bright-shiny-object syndrome is everything you see on social media, the free webinars, gifts, training courses, coaching programes, books, podcasts—the list is endless. Know what you need and why you need it and avoid everything else. If you need a coach or mentor, get *one*, not five. If you need help with marketing, know what you need and why you need it and follow one thing, not multiple. You would only have one accountant; you don't need more information, more help, or more shiny objects.

The more bright shiny objects you have the more you will be distracted, the more you will procrastinate, and the more you will not be doing what you need to be doing.

As an entrepreneur you should be doing two things:

- Growing your business
- Creating relationships (Selling)

That's it—my magic recipe. Yes there are the things I mentioned in the introduction but really, that's it. All of the admin is growing the business, as you need to know where you are and where you need to go. Content creation or product creation is growing, everything else is selling.

Focus what you are doing and when you are doing it and ideally do not spend any longer than 90 minutes on any one task at a time. Our brains will only focus for 90 minutes at a time and after that we need a break, we need to walk away; take 10 or 15 minutes to recharge and refocus and then move on.

If you have sat through a three-hour film or an all-day meeting and you feel your energy and your concentration flagging you will know what I mean.

As an entrepreneur your mindset is vital. If you see failure and despair you will receive failure and despair; if you see clients, money, and growth, guess what you will receive?

I practice gratitude daily. I have a gratitude jar that I write little notes for every day of what I am grateful for. I file all of my testimonials and e-mails of thanks into a folder in my e-mail called "Happy" and refer back to it when I need a boost. I keep the cards I receive from clients on a shelf in my office to remind me of the lives I have changed.

Remember to take time and celebrate your successes, every single one—no matter how small. You will find the more you do this the more success you will have. If you pass over the good things and think "it wasn't enough," or you move straight onto the next thing, you will never really find true happiness in yourself or your business.

Top Tips

- Be grateful
- Celebrate success

- Carve your diary into 90-minute blocks
- Stay focused
- Have fun

Mindset: Generalist or Specialist?

I Don't Have A Niche!!

At school I was good at a lot of things, but never excelled in anything. I had a lot of interests but not a main passion. Throughout my career I have been good at lots of things but never a specialist in anything. Because of this I can easily get sidetracked and I have to keep moving forward and remember to focus on what I am doing.

When I started my HR career I was a generalist—I liked doing everything. I specialized in leadership development and training for a while but found doing just one thing didn't excite me and light me up in the same way , so I went back to being a generalist. I like the variety.

When I started my first company, I advertised as a Coach and Consultant. At many networking events I was always told I needed a niche; I couldn't decide on one thing.

I started to learn more about Neuroscience and Mindset and used these as tools to deepen all aspects of my work, but the more I learned about mindset, the more I have continued to develop in this area. It has taken me away from my purpose, and in fact it has provided greater benefit to all aspects of my work, including my HR practice, as I now feed neuroscience into HR to help businesses learn how to better lead, engage, and motivate their employees.

My Virgo Buddy, the teenage daughter of a friend of mine who I share my birthday with, was also confused as she doesn't have a specialism and feels she needs one to finish secondary school so she can pick a job when she leaves school. The truth is she is great at everything and totally awesome at art, yet she didn't choose art as a topic to study because she doesn't create art in the way her school expects—she says she can't draw faces. Ludicrous, isn't it?

Society tells us we need a specialism so we sit in the same box as everyone else.

Despite being appointed as the UK's youngest HR Director, I don't tick a lot of the HR boxes as I don't have one specific strength, usually ER or Change; yet the truth is, I did this day in and day out and if some of the recruiters I worked with over the years had bothered to have a conversation with me about this, they would have realized that I can cover all of the aspects required.

I love working with mindset. I'm not saying that mindset alone is enough to create transformational change, but it's certainly a great place to start.

Boxes, labels, and niches have their place, but if you are a generalist, or as I call myself, jack-of-all-trades and master of many, embrace it. Don't limit yourself or your skills or your passions because someone tells you that you have to just to market yourself more effectively or be able to find one job that more closely matches the one skill you have.

When the time is right, and when people need what you have, they will find you and no clever or expensive marketing campaign is going to help with that. My website needs an overhaul, but for now, it's good enough, people are finding me and my team and I would rather be working with my amazing clients than sat staring at a website. It will happen, but for now, it's fine.

In truth, the more things you can find that you love doing and that match your skills, passions, or values, the greater your scope for growth and living a wholehearted life to help you develop and grow a successful career.

And if you do have that "one thing," that's OK too, but don't assume that everyone around you will just have one thing or try to insist that they have one.

Intellect will only get you so far. I know a few people who have achieved the highest grades at "A" level only to be told by leading universities that because of their inability to engage and communicate with others they are not what the university is looking for.

Embrace your skills and your talents and your differences, all of them, no matter how many you have.

Top Tips

- Understand all of your skills, strengths, and passions and find a role where you can embrace as many of these as possible.

- Don't let anyone push you down a rabbit hole because it suits them.
- Recognize that one path doesn't have to be the only path.

Mindset and (Work) Life Balance

Work-life balance is a concept including proper prioritization between "work" (career and ambition) and "lifestyle" (health, pleasure, leisure, family, and spiritual development/meditation).

I looked at the definition above and struggled. "Proper prioritization," what on earth does that mean? Mostly, family is our biggest priority—whether you are married, have kids, or are a carer, family comes first. But career and ambition is what keeps the roof over your head, pays your bills, funds your lifestyle, and supports your leisure time; so how do you properly prioritize that?

First (and although I mention the term *work-life* throughout the book), I believe there is only life balance. To separate work from life is like saying that work isn't part of life, and actually it is, a big part. Most of us will work for more than half our lives, we spend most of our week at work or working, and it's a fundamental and important part of life. Plus, if you work full-time then your week is out of balance time-wise before you even try and start fitting anything else in.

As a mum, I have never missed a sports day (that's a lie, I missed one that was rearranged that my Mum and Dad went to instead), I have never missed an assembly, an awards evening, or a parents evening, and I always help with homework. I have taken time away from work when my parents have been ill or friends have needed me. I walk the dog daily, I meditate daily, I journal regularly. I spend time with my partner, meet up with friends, exercise, enjoy life, and work hard. Do I always get it right? Honestly, I have no idea.

I've not always been home for dinner or bedtime, I'm not always about in the evenings or every weekend, and I've spent nights away working or on courses. I do this to provide for my sons, to keep a roof over our heads, and to keep my businesses going. Now my sons' dad and I are no longer together; we coparent and the boys split their week between us both. I try as much as I can to keep evening appointments for when my sons are with their dad, while still spending time with my partner, so I'm there when the boys are home.

The one thing that does go out of the window for me, when I'm out of balance, is exercise. I either sleep for longer in the morning and miss my morning routine, or work into the evening and miss my evening routine. I walk as much as I can, but doing work that mostly involves sitting (although I do stand and work a lot), if I don't exercise, I'm not really moving at all. I've contemplated a running machine desk but multitasking takes my attention from the thing I'm meant to be doing so I couldn't guarantee the quality of anything I would produce. Although I would love to hear from anyone who has one so I know if they actually work.

I know that exercise is important, as is eating healthily, but if I'm "prioritizing properly," my family and my work come first. I do spend time on myself, for myself, and have my daily meditation ritual, but if I have to choose between kids and exercise, sleep and exercise, or work and exercise, the exercise goes out of the window.

I prioritize things based on my purpose. Always family first, and then I'm back to helping others grow, so work will always come next. I have two questions I ask myself when making decisions and prioritizing, "Is this going to help me achieve my purpose?" and "Is it a priority right now?" If the answer to any of these questions is anything but yes, I don't do it.

We constantly talk about work-life balance and how it seems to be the "holy grail" of all life has to offer. I know people who work a four-day week to spend a full day with kids or to get to the gym, I know people that play golf every Tuesday, I know people that only work until 2 p.m. every day, I know people that work while travelling, and I know people who work 12 hours a day seven days a week and take all summer off work. For all of them this is balance.

What does balance mean to you?

How will you know when you have achieved it?

And how will you "properly prioritize?"

Top Tips

- Be clear in your own mind what balance means to you.
- Find a balance that works for you—if something isn't working make a change.
- Forget about creating work-life balance, and focus on a balanced life.

Mindset and Confidence

confidence

noun

the feeling or belief that one can have faith in or rely on someone or something.

Can you rely on you? Do you have faith in you?

I'm taking a guess here, but if you are reading these questions and looking at it from the perspective of other people being able to rely on you and your ability to do something that you said you would to help someone else, that you answered yes to both of these questions.

If I rephrase the questions and ask if you have confidence in your ability to succeed or gain a promotion or step out of your comfort zone, is your answer the same?

Confidence was a big stepping stone for me and is one of the biggest hurdles for many of my clients, either because of something that someone else has told us we aren't good enough at, because of an experience, or just because our inner voice is telling us we aren't good enough.

At a time when I was having hypnotherapy sessions, the therapist asked me if my inner voice was saying "I" or "you." At the time I thought it was the same thing, and because the voice was in my head, when it was saying "you" can't do that, it was talking from me, to me.

What he told me was that, if the voice in my head was saying "I," it was *my* own belief stopping me and holding me back. If my inner voice was saying "you," it was coming from someone at some point or another in my life telling me I couldn't do something.

My voice said *you*. Instantly I knew who it was. It was the mum of one of my primary-school friends who saw me as a threat to her daughter and told me, my parents, and my teachers that I wasn't as good as her daughter. As it turned out, I was. Yet the voice, her voice, had subconsciously stuck with me for over 30 years.

You'll see from some of the case studies in Part 3 that confidence (along with fear) comes up frequently as the one thing that holds us back the most.

Most of the people that I work with as their coach, and who have issues with confidence, have been crushed by colleagues, mainly by managers, and now lack the confidence to move on. They struggle to move on because they have been told they aren't good enough, they have been told they have failed, or they have been overlooked and made to feel worthless. They haven't been given this information constructively, or supported or developed to stop them being so "terrible" at their job; they have just been crushed and left to pick up the pieces on their own.

In Part 3, Case Studies, you will find some case studies about people I spoke to about their struggles specifically for this book, and confidence (or lack of it) was the biggest thing holding them back.

Visualize a typical day in your life.

Where are you?

What are you doing?

Wherever you are and whatever you are doing you are happy and you are doing everything brilliantly. You are the most competent, confident, successful person in the room.

And then in I walk and tell you you're none of those things. I belittle you or challenge you, I tell you I'm better, I tell everyone else I'm better, I go behind your back telling friends, family, or colleagues that you are no good, and I do this repeatedly. And you start to believe it.

You believe you aren't good enough because why would I say that about you if it weren't true? You start to doubt everything you are doing and everything you are saying and when an opportunity comes along for you to show how good you are, you don't take it, because you've now told yourself and begun to believe that you aren't good enough.

The voice in your head then tells you to doubt anything and everything and you start to sink, never pushing, never moving forward because you'll "only fail if you do."

Unfortunately this happens at work, at home, and at schools, and we have to stop it.

I may be better than you at some things but, I guarantee you, not everything, and in any case, where I am "better," you will do it differently and it may work in a different way. There will always be someone better, taller, stronger, faster, prettier, brighter—the list here is ridiculously long again. But if you are confident enough in your own abilities and strengths you don't see those who are better as competition—it becomes collaboration or just wills you to do better and continue to grow.

I'm a coach. If I believe I'm not good enough, and it's a crowded market, guess what? I find no clients, believe I'm not good enough, and end up with no clients and no money. If I believe there are loads of coaches and we all provide something different to clients and that the clients I work with have chosen me because I'm the best fit for them, I end up working with clients who I am the best fit for.

Don't get me wrong, a lot of my work is referral based and my marketing doesn't always bring me all of the clients I would like, but the right clients come at the right time. If I give up at the first hurdle, I will never achieve what I want to achieve. I have to be confident in my own abilities. And if I'm not, how can I truly be an authentic coach?

You may know some inauthentic people in your company. They talk about the right way to do it, the best way to lead and manage, and then they do the exact opposite. They don't exactly fill you with confidence or inspire you to do your job. do they? No.

Get clear on your strengths, and talk to your inner voice when doubt starts to creep in. Increase your confidence by being comfortable with who you are, what you do, what you say, and how you act. This isn't about becoming arrogant or egotistical but being confident in yourself and your own abilities so that others can't knock it out of you.

Money Mindset

As I sit writing this chapter, I'm not writing as a self-made millionaire sitting on pots of cash. I know the money is on its way, I know what I need to do to make it happen, I know where it's coming from, how much

I have in the bank, how much I have invested and how much I want for the future.

I have, however, changed my thinking and my perception of money, and it is this along with my own story and experiences that I share with you in this chapter.

Money is not something that has grown on trees in my life, and it has often burnt a hole in my pocket. Until recently I have had a terrible relationship with money all of my life and it has taken me years to truly understand why and to develop a money mindset.

As a child I never went without anything. I may have had to wait for some items to come to me at birthdays or Christmas but eventually I would always get what I wanted.

Whenever I asked for anything, my parents would constantly tell me that money didn't grow on trees, and without even realizing it, I was forming a thinking pattern and a mindset that in order to have money you *had* to work hard for it.

"Rich" people were few and far between and "not everyone" could have it all was what I had engrained in my mind.

I started earning money when I was 12. I had a part-time job after school and at weekends in a fruit-and-vegetable shop earning £2 an hour. I was paid cash each week and used this money to treat my friends and I started to buy my own clothes, the nonessential items. My Mum would always try and encourage me to save money, but I never did.

I continued to work part-time throughout my education and as quickly as I earned it I spent it, and as I got older more of my money was spent on socializing and nights out and of course the outfits to go out in.

At aged 14 I took myself to the hairdresser's for a new cut and style and the follow-on cuts for the upkeep once a month.

I started driving at 17; my parents bought me first car, my second, and my third, and my money then went on petrol. Friends would occasionally offer petrol money for driving them round but I rarely accepted it.

One of my friends would always ask the rest of the group for change to buy another drink, which we gave, only to find out he had asked to save him breaking a note. We saw him as "tight" rather than frugal, and even today, he will be the last one to get a round of drinks in or dig in to split the taxi fare.

At the age of 18 I was offered credit cards and loans that I took and at the time I was having my rent paid for by my employer. My salary was therefore all about spending—I was still not in the mindset of saving.

I spent the next 12 years in and out of debt, spending what I had as quickly as possible and then struggling to pay bills and live for the rest of the month, so I borrowed. Money had destroyed some personal friendships and relationships and still I couldn't break the cycle.

I was earning a six-figure salary before I started my own business and while I was generating income, in many ways the money coming in was spent before it arrived in my account on the house, holidays, cars, clothes, handbags, or treats for my sons.

In 2013 I read and watched *The Secret*, and was able to manifest a convertible Mercedes. I say manifest it. I read the book, visualized the car, and while my then husband and I were out looking for vans for him, we spotted an SLK and bought that instead. BUT having never had money saved, I couldn't imagine what it would be like to have money in the bank (despite the large figure that entered my account each month), and while I tried to manifest it, I always had the thought that it would never happen, and it didn't.

I knew something needed to change, but I still didn't know how to make it happen. Following some health issues I really started to struggle financially. I had almost six months of living hand to mouth, wondering how I would pay my team, my bills, and my rent and even how I would buy food. I had the hardest Christmas I had ever had wondering how I would buy presents for my sons, and I felt awful.

Something had to change, but what?

I strongly believe that we each have the resources within to help us move forward in life and live the life we want, yet I had constantly been looking outward when it came to money. Aware that there are money coaches out there, I read books, watched webinars, and completed training, but nothing was changing.

I then received a letter saying I may be made bankrupt as I hadn't been able to keep up a payment from a debt of my husband's over the last six months. I started to go into a well of despair and then thought that a clean slate may actually do me some good. For the first time in my life, I realized it was a new financial day, a new opportunity to start over and that I thought that some good would come from this.

I sat and completed some of my mindset exercises and discovered some of my blockages.

I had grown up thinking that money was hard to come by. I had grown up thinking that you had to work your fingers to the bone to earn a living and the money to go with it. I had also been "taught" that there wasn't enough money for everyone. Coming from a working-class family where there was only ever "just enough to go round" and regular arguments about money, this had become part of my life.

And there I was with my clean slate and my fresh outlook and no longer worried about money despite the threat of bankruptcy.

I told myself that in that month I would generate £30,000 of income, that by the end of the month I would have £30,000 in the bank. That would cover wages for a couple of months and allow me to pay my bills.

I invoiced £24,500 that month. I didn't beat myself up that it wasn't the £30K I had thought of; I just set a bigger target for the following month, £50,000.

I invoiced £49,000 that month, again not quite my target but I couldn't complain at all. I was generating revenue, I was invoicing, and I was getting myself back on track. Now all I needed was one bigger contract and that would pay wages for the year, pay off my bills, and allow me to start saving, but I would have to keep the purse strings as tight as I had for the last six months.

I was budgeting for the first time ever, saving money and watching money grow, overcoming my previous thought patterns, and making it happen.

I invoiced £120,000 for three consecutive months and I was in the clear.

I'm now focused on £5,000,000 in 12 months. It's saved on the screensaver on my laptop and written on blank checks on my fridge and in my office. I don't know where it's coming from or how it will get there, but I know it's out there for the taking and that I will get it.

I've broken the cycle, changed my mindset, and set myself free.

Top Tips

- Know what your views of money are
- Know and understand your relationship with money

- Set clear intentions
- Focus on the positives

"Not Enough Time" Mindset

You're busy?

Not enough hours in the day?

Running round in circles?

Know how to manage your time but can't seem to be able to make it work?

It's time to manage your time by focusing on your purpose.

Now many of us have attended courses, read books, or attended seminars on how to manage time, but we are in a bit of a vicious circle, because most of the time we don't create the time to put into practice what we have learned. And the longer we leave it, the harder it is to make the changes we need to make.

So what's the answer?

My first book, *Create Your Purpose, Manage Your Time*, focuses on seven key areas of focus that, if followed, will make a massive impact on how you manage your time.

Here, I provide just a short summary of these seven steps to get the wheels in motion and help you change your mindset from "not enough time," to "more than enough time."

Remember it's all about our beliefs.

So, my seven proven tips are:

1. Know your why: Be clear on your purpose and know what you are trying to or wanting to achieve.
2. Know your strategy: When you are clear on your why and your purpose you can create a clear strategy to help you achieve it. Whether it's a vision board, a list of priorities, or an action plan, create your strategy and stick to it. Your strategy should focus on your why or you will just continue to run round in circles.
3. Know your mindset: Listen to your heart more than your head. Go with your gut. Be clear on which part of your brain you are operating

from at any given time; listen out for your fixed mindset and challenge it with your growth mindset. Turn any negative thoughts into positive thoughts.

4. Know what's in your toolbox: Know who and what you have at your disposal that you can make full use of to help you achieve your strategy and accomplish your why. This can be people, equipment, knowledge, or skills—the list is endless. Your toolbox needs to be full of things that will help you achieve your strategy and realize your vision.

5. Know who and what gives you energy: I call these your Energy Vampires and your Energy Angels. Vampires are things or people that drain you of energy—mine are spreadsheets, inauthentic people, the news, trash TV, and carbs. Energy Angels are things or people that fill you with energy—mine are creating or facilitating workshops, helping others, my family, friends and team, inspirational people, Yoga, cycling, and veggies. On average you need a ratio of 3:1, Angels to Vampires. Surround yourself with as many Angels as you can.

6. Know who you are accountable to: When you are clear on your why, your strategy, your mindset, and your tools, it's time to get clear on who you are accountable to. This could be customers, your team, family, or friends. Even if you run your own business you are accountable to someone. Get them clear in your head as this will help you prioritize where you need to focus your time and attention based on your strategy and your why.

7. Know what you can say no to: Many find this the hardest thing to do, but in some ways it's the most important. If you continue to say yes when you should be saying no, you are filling your diary with things that will not help you reach your why and achieve your vision. I use two qualifying questions—"Is this a priority right now?" and "Will this help me achieve my why?" If the answer to any of these is *no* or *maybe*, I don't do it. By saying no and managing your time you are creating more space for *yes*!

Make the most of every day and every opportunity. Don't waste time—it's too precious.

"If—"
Rudyard Kipling

If you can keep your head when all about you
Are losing theirs and blaming it on you,
If you can trust yourself when all men doubt you,
But make allowance for their doubting too;
If you can wait and not be tired of waiting,
Or being lied about, don't deal in lies,
Or being hated, don't give way to hating,
And yet don't look too good, nor talk too wise:

If you can dream—and not make dreams your master;
If you can think—and not make thoughts your aim;
If you can meet with Triumph and Disaster
And treat those two impostors just the same;
If you can bear to hear the truth you've spoken
Twisted by knaves to make a trap for fools,
Or watch the things you gave your life to, broken,
And stoop and build 'em up with worn-out tools:

If you can make one heap of all your winnings
And risk it on one turn of pitch-and-toss,
And lose, and start again at your beginnings
And never breathe a word about your loss;
If you can force your heart and nerve and sinew
To serve your turn long after they are gone,
And so hold on where there is nothing in you
Except the Will which says to them: "Hold on!"

If you can talk with crowds and keep your virtue,
Or walk with Kings—nor lose the common touch,
If neither foes nor loving friends can hurt you,
If all men count with you, but none too much;
If you can fill the unforgiving minute
With sixty seconds' worth of distance run,
Yours is the Earth and everything that's in it,
And—which is more—you'll be a Man, my son!

Recruitment and Mindset

When you are on the career ladder, whether looking for internal promotions or seeking jobs in other companies, you will no doubt have to endure a recruitment process of some kind.

This may involve a straightforward interview, perhaps a more informal chat, an assessment center, a technical assessment, or, if you are applying for a role with Disney, maybe an audition.

Over the years I have seen many candidates, who seem to be the best person on paper, crumble when it comes to the interview process. Why?

Mindset.

But sometimes, even before the interview process, mindset can get in the way when it comes to applying for roles or going for a promotion in the first place. And this is the biggest obstacle for some when it comes to mastering a mindset for career success.

You've been doing really well in your role, you're ready for a new challenge, and you want to move to the next stage of your career. You start looking for opportunities that meet your requirements and suit your skillset. You find a role with the right salary and the stretch you want, and you polish up your CV ready to apply for the role.

Here's another difference between the genders when it comes to moving up. Women tend to apply for the role when they feel they can meet between 80 and 100 percent of the requirements of the role. Men tend to apply when they feel can do between 50 and 60 percent of the role. The difference in the method of applying, therefore, is not so much based on skill, but on the difference between the male and the female brain and how the genders are able to adapt their CV to meet the requirements of the role.

In reality, if you wait until you can do 100 percent of the role, then there is no stretch for you, because in actual fact what you are applying for is the role that you already have. A new role will always be a challenge, a new company will always be a challenge, there will always be new things to learn, and you just have to get on and learn them.

There will be people that you can call on for help, advice, and support, and *nobody* is amazing at everything.

Enough with the Labels

My team and I are qualified and experienced in the use and feedback methods of a number of psychometric tests and, as with everything, these types of assessments have their place, but isn't it time we stopped this?

There appears to be an increasing number of adverts being placed for jobs all seeking "red" applicants, which to me seems bizarre. Recruiters seem to be narrowing searches enough at the minute by demanding a certain sector or a certain number of years of experience (and roles remain unfilled, really!!).

Over the years we have seen psychometrics used to give people jobs, or not, to give promotions or not, but perhaps the most disturbing trend is that they are used by lazy managers to excuse behavior. Yes, really, there are some lazy managers out there!

What do we mean by this?

Well, whatever the letter, the color, the number, or the pack, psychometric tests highlight both strong and developmental areas in a person.

One company had a sales director who upset his entire team, couldn't work as part of a team, was rude, opinionated, refused to share information, spent a lot of time on breaks, but hit his sales targets. His behavior was excused by his line manager because it had all shown up as part of his test and therefore they knew to expect this from him. Yet he was damaging the confidence of many of his team members, alienating his peers, and causing friction every time he walked into a room.

In another company a head of service was constantly receiving complaints from customers and grievances from members of his team. The director excused his behavior because it had showed in his psychometric that he couldn't relate to people.

In another company you didn't get through to the final stage of the interview unless you had a certain score on one of these tests. Candidates rarely got through to the third stage and those that did and were hired barely made it through their probation period.

Regardless of what a test says, it does not excuse this type of behavior, not in a company that wants to succeed anyway. If we want to grow and develop, we need to focus on three core areas; language, relationships, and behaviors. What do people say, how do they interact, and how do they behave? These three areas impact performance and culture more than anything else in a business, yet so often we overlook them and base decisions on statistics and testing.

So let's get back to speaking and connecting with people, removing labels and testing, and actually working with people for what they really are—people! Let's change the mindset of recruiting managers and recruiters.

So you've applied for the role, you've passed the "test," and you've been offered an interview. Now you need to control your mindset. (At the end of the book you'll find the Jen and Sally case study that will show you the power of mindset when under pressure.)

The language we use is important to creating and maintaining a positive mindset. "I'm so nervous" will only fuel more feelings of nervousness. "I'm looking forward to talking about my achievements and my desires for my career development" is just one way to frame the language you use and prepare yourself for the interview.

If you need to travel for the interview, allow plenty of time, you don't want to get caught in traffic, and ideally, before you enter the building you want to go somewhere to grab 10 or 15 minutes to yourself where you can grab a drink, take some deep breaths, repeat some positive affirmations, and then head in, prepared and ready to secure you job. Remember to visit the bathroom, check your appearance in the mirror, and ensure you have nothing stuck in your teeth or spilled down your top.

When you arrive, don't sit looking at your phone. Stay focused on the interview that you are about to enter rather than your latest e-mails or social media updates. You don't want your positivity being overshadowed by the white noise of the outside world; this is your time. Plus, if the interviewer knows you have arrived and calls you in early, or they are running slightly late, you want to show that your only focus is the interview. I do not like having to wait for candidates to turn off their phone; it makes me feel they are not interested.

In the interview itself, listen to the questions. I've sat opposite so many candidates who are reciting what they have prepared in their head before the interview rather than listening to and answering the questions being asked.

Use positive language and refer to "I" rather than "we." Your team is not being interviewed, *you* are. If you are asked a question about something you have no experience of, but want to learn it, or are willing to learn it, don't start telling the panel that you don't know. Give a positive example of something similar, talk about your learning style. This isn't about lying, though.

Have questions prepared and ask them. Don't focus on money; focus on the role, the development opportunities, the culture, the environment; ask the interviewers what they love about the company and why they have stayed. Interviews are two-way processes.

You've been offered the job, you've agreed on your salary and start date, and the first day of your job has arrived.

How are you feeling? Remember, positive words and language help you manage your mindset in fostering a career for success.

An added tip: how people perceive you will be based on four things—your appearance (sorry but it's true—it shouldn't be, but it is), your language, your relationships, and your behavior. Don't try and be anything you're not, but be conscious of the way you are presenting yourself and the confidence with which you do it.

Top Tips

- If the role calls out to you, apply for it, regardless of how much of it you can do.
- Deep breathing helps you relax.
- Positive self-talk and language improves self-confidence.
- First impressions count; stay off your phone, be presentable, consider how you act, interact, speak, and behave.

Mindset and Glass Ceilings

Glass Ceiling

noun

An unacknowledged barrier to advancement in a profession, especially affecting women and members of minorities.

The first time I was asked to deliver at a women's network was on the topic of Glass Ceilings and the issues I had faced throughout my career in competing with men. I explained I had never encountered this issue but I could give my opinion on the differences between men and women when seeking a new role or a promotion from an HR perspective.

Typically, women will wait until they can do 100 percent of the role outlined in the job description, whereas men will typically apply if they can do 60 percent of the role.

Men talk in interviews about "I" and women focus on "we."

Research has demonstrated that throughout school females outperform males; we work hard and receive recognition through the grades we receive. When we enter the world of work we assume our efforts will continue to be rewarded in the same way, and for some this is the case, but for many, our efforts may go unnoticed because we aren't talking about our successes and showcasing our talents in order to get the recognition we deserve.

The definition of the Glass Ceiling, as we see above, is an invisible barrier. I always believed I could achieve whatever I wanted to, and so far I haven't proven myself wrong. Don't get me wrong but there are still some organizations out there where glass ceilings are a reality. You need to be in the "club" in order to get promoted or recognized, but this is changing.

In some cases, the glass ceiling is a figment of our imagination; however, once we have set the limit and told ourselves that it's there, we start to believe it. Once that belief is engrained in our minds, our language, our relationships, and our behaviors start to reflect this and we begin to display resentment and bitterness.

Another concept is the "Glass Cliff" and this typically refers to women who have made it to the top but due to lack of time, support, or resources are quickly pushed off, whereas males at the top appear to be given longer, with more money and additional resources to "fix the issue." At this point, we see women jumping before they are pushed and moving onto roles in smaller companies or leaving to start their own businesses.

I have been lucky to have so many inspirational female role models in my life, at home, at school, in education, and at work. I attend events with inspirational female speakers who have made it to the top and are succeeding in their roles. My network is filled with inspirational successful women. The great coaches and mentors I have worked with have been inspirational successful women. No ceilings, just striving for and reaching success (although we all have different views on what success looks like).

In 2013 I was at a two-day development workshop where at the end of the first day there was a panel discussion. One panel member stood out for me as she told her story. She worked in London and had just been made partner in a large consultancy firm. And she was the first woman to do so. She had worked hard, broken the ceiling, and achieved what she wanted to achieve. She did speak about the "boys' club" and some of the nights out where she felt like an outcast because she wasn't engaging in brandy and cigars, but she had been recognized for her skills, talent, and hard work and had "made it."

In 2014 I attended an event with 300 women at the London Business School where there were a host of fantastic female speakers, all of whom were either CEOs or members of boards in international and global companies. The common theme they all spoke about was working hard to encourage more women into senior positions as they acted as role models to show it could be done.

Two speakers displayed their frustration at questions from the audience about juggling motherhood with a career. They both responded by asking if questions of fatherhood would have been posed to male speakers; the answer, no.

Throughout my career I have worked hard to remove barriers and boxes from the workplace. Our own beliefs can hinder us as can psychometric testing that excuses our behaviors or limits our growth—that is, "they act like that because they are … ," "you'll never be able to achieve that because you are …"

I hold a strong belief that we each hold the answers and the resources within us to achieve what we want to achieve. If we want to aim high, we should stop thinking of barriers, stop boxing ourselves in with labels and stereotypes, and just be ourselves.

After all, you are what you think.

3 Tips to Breaking the Glass Ceiling

- act like there are no barriers, boxes, labels, or limits
- believe in yourself and your own ability
- find an amazing coach or mentor to get you to the next level

"Until You Do"
Rosemary Dun (2005)

There are monsters by my bed growling. Because once upon a time I let them in and had two beautiful babies that I picked up, one under each arm, and fled through the woods to a place where there stood ramshackle and not very nice houses. That would do. That were better, At least I could try and cover the cracks and block up the holes where the monsters poked their snouts through to snuffle at the pretty babies.

But in time, the wolves turned up. Huffing and puffing they threatened to blow all the houses down And one by one the houses did come down but each time I built stronger, and better houses. One of straw, one of sticks, and finally one of bricks which had no gaps in the stripped floors nor any holes in the skirting boards.

The babies grew into beautiful yet watchful adults And one cloaked herself in fear to guard against the monsters; while the other stopped up her ears and donned the best armour she could make out of stories, and bravery.

But it was no good. The monsters still lurked by the side of my wardrobe, still came at night to tug at our bedclothes and scratch at our dreams. Until one day, I shone a torch on those monsters which lurked. I shone the beam on their lying hiding hidey-hole. And they went away Success occurs when your dreams get bigger than your excuses

Mindset and Development

You've got the job, you're loving it, you don't want to stop learning. How do you keep developing? First consider again whether you have a growth mindset or a fixed mindset as this may determine what you learn and the way you learn it.

I have lost track of the time and money I have spent on my personal and professional development over the years, and my employers have also supported me a great deal. I'm a lifelong learner, I love learning, and I start each day and enter into every new situation with the aim of learning at least one new thing. Just one thing every day means that by the end of the year I will have learned 365 new things.

If we are open enough to learning, we can indeed pick things up from anyone and anywhere to help us develop our career. But first you have to be open. I've met so many people over the years who, with their fixed mindset, are convinced that they know it all. They see no value in coaching, reading, courses, workshops, qualifications, degrees, learning from others. They feel they know it all and that nobody can teach them anything (they haven't moved forward with their career in years), and, don't get me wrong, sometimes we do know what someone is teaching us or saying to us, but we can learn how to see things from their perspective instead of our own.

And sometimes we outgrow a certain way of learning, or we need to move our development to the next level, or we need to work with someone who is at another level so that we can learn from them.

Development, be it personal or professional, doesn't always have to cost a lot, and it doesn't always need to consume a lot of our time. It's not always about MBAs and degrees, we can learn from everyone around us, and with such a wealth of books, online programs, seminars, TED talks, YouTube videos, and Google searches, the world of development is at our fingertips, if we are open to learning.

Figure 2.1 below shows some of the statistics about learning retention, details of which many learning institutions and workplaces ignore when it comes to ensuring that the learners retain and are able to embed what they have learned.

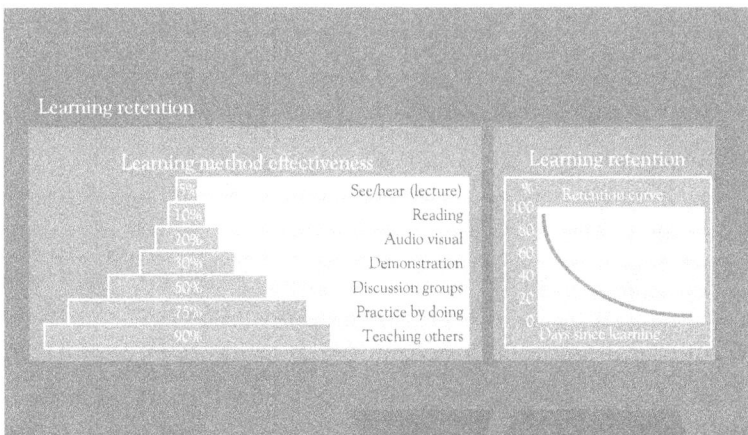

Figure 2.1 Learning retention

Only five percent of what we learn comes from what we see and hear, whereas 90 percent comes from learning when we teach others. And when it comes to how long we retain information for, we forget, or lose, 80 percent of what we are taught if we don't implement it within six days of learning it.

Every year, millions of pounds are spent on learning and development; what we don't invest so much in, is embedding and retaining the knowledge. If you want to continue to develop in your career, you need to find a way to learn that suits you, and you need to create the time and space to reflect on and embed the learning.

Whenever I'm coaching or running a workshop, I always encourage participants to plan time after the session to reflect on what they have learned. I then encourage them to take some time to plan how they can implement the learning within the next 24 hours and make a commitment to doing so. "I commit to . . . in the next 24 hours" is a powerful statement. It affirms to the conscious and subconscious mind that change is going to happen and it sets a timeframe for this.

If I'm facilitating a workshop I add one more point to this also, and again ask for a commitment from them, once again to embed the learning, and that is "who will you teach what you have learned today and by when?" Knowing that 90 percent of learning retention comes from teaching others, this is another way to ensure the learning is embedded. Now this could be just sharing it with your partner or kids when you get home. It could be leading a team meeting and sharing it with your colleagues, it could be writing a blog post and sharing it with people in your network, but if you want to grow and develop, you need to programe your mind in ways that help you learn and retain the information.

Many authors now have Facebook groups or forums on websites or other social media platforms set up for their readers. First, of course, this helps from a marketing perspective to sell additional content and books, but it also encourages people to share what they have learned and how they have implemented it. And if people are sharing what they have learned and implementing it to help them be more successful, then not only is the learning taking place, but the readers become amazing advocates for promoting your book to others.

We have all bought or read books that sit on the shelf unread, or that you read and then put straight back down again with no mention of it to anyone, but if you really, truly learned from it, you will share this with others. And it's similar with TED talks. Two of my favorites are Brené Brown and Simon Sinek, who are probably like a lot of other people, but they convey messages that get people talking and learning and doing things differently, and being successful. A series of workshops I run specifically for women in business use a lot of the Dove Real Beauty campaign videos. And I know that many of the women from the workshops have gone on to share these with others. Watching a video is one thing, but we have to implement the change.

I know someone who is constantly completing degree, after degree, after degree. They are very intelligent and very knowledgeable, but only from a theoretical and textbook sense. When it comes to implementing any of what they have learned, they can't put it into practice, or think outside the box, or find solutions, or in some cases even demonstrate any common sense.

If we don't implement and embed what we learn, then we will struggle to foster a mindset for career success.

Consider what you want to learn and why you want to learn it and implement the learning within 24 hours. Create the implementation of your learning as a new pattern and through process in your brain where it becomes habit.

Top Tips

- Consider further whether you have a growth or a fixed mindset
- Aim to learn one new thing each day
- Commit to and create time for embedding learning through teaching others

Mindset and Change: Animal Instincts and Primitive Brains

Change, as we know, is fast becoming one of the only constants in business so you would think that the process, the feelings, and the outcomes would be much easier for us all to deal with. But this isn't the case.

I've been thinking about this a lot over the last few months, and animals and primitive brains came to mind. Let's explore this.

A change is announced at work: a merger, an acquisition, or employee cuts for efficiencies or cost saving. At first, although shocked (maybe), you deal with it and feel OK. Then the jungle drums start thudding and you notice panic setting in. Behaviors change, gossip starts, and you too start to change the way you feel about the change and about your ability.

Ordinarily you know you are good at your job and you hope you will be OK. You'll wait and see what happens, and if you do have to leave you can do so with some money in your pocket and find a new job, start your own business, or take the opportunity to learn some new skills and start a new career path. You are still feeling quite calm.

And then it starts.

People around you are starting to belittle each other, "I'm better than you." In meetings or during work people are stamping all over each other, shouting loudest, "pick me, pick me, you need me you know you do," and then you begin to wonder why you would want to stay working with people that would do this to each other and "is this a culture I want to stay in any longer?"

So why is all of this happening?

When we become fearful of a situation we tend to work from the primitive part of our brains and repeat primitive behaviors and patterns. Male colleagues tend to jump into "protector" mode, having to feed and hunt and gather and start to display behavior that puts them in the Alpha Male spot. And all of a sudden the female employees are surrounded by peacocks, lions, and wolves.

There can only be one male in the pack and so the fight begins. The peacocks start fanning their feathers to show who has the brightest display and the wolves start to break up the pack. The office becomes filled with howling, roaring, and feathers as the males in the group try to display their inner alpha male, eager to survive the change and fearful of what people will think of them if they don't survive the change.

Women see the displays and the roaring and the howling and think, "I don't like that behavior," and we let the men fight it out, hoping that our credibility and integrity will be enough to get us through the change.

We become insular, avoiding as much as possible the testosterone around us and then we start to doubt ourselves, our skills, and our future and wonder what we will do next if we don't survive the process.

By and large, because women like don't the atmosphere that has been created at work, we start to see ourselves in different jobs, maybe starting our own business, although "that seems quite scary and I don't know if I could do that" because confidence levels are at an all-time low.

Whether male or female or how much you love the job, and until recently you loved the company, but "I can't stay in this environment, although can I really afford to leave?" And you sit and wait, hoping that everything will work out well and that you don't really need to make a decision because it will be made for you. "If I get a job in the new structure then great, and if not I'll find something else."

You become the shoulder for your colleagues to lean on because you are seen to be quiet and composed and everyone wants to know how you are staying so calm, but they continue to make digs at you during the conversation to demonstrate that they "really" are better than you in the hope that you too will start to crumble. You smile nicely, carry on working, and wait until you are home with a glass of wine before letting all of your emotions out. You are now in your primitive brain and blending into the background like a peahen.

Top Tips

- Believe in yourself—create a "change" affirmation that reminds you of your greatness
- The animals will self-select—focus on yourself
- If you must step into the lion's den, claim your spot as the Alpha in an authentic, credible, and nice way—no need for claws or feathers.

Why We Can Find Change Difficult

Sometimes we initiate the change and sometimes it is forced upon us, sometimes the change is slow and sometimes it moves at 100 miles an hour.

Why do we often find it so hard, whatever the change and whatever the pace? Why does some change fill us with delight and others fill us with dread?

Well, first of all, there is a bit of science behind it. The saying "we are creatures of habit" is in fact very true. As we move through life we develop beliefs, thoughts, and patterns in the primitive part of our brain and when faced with a "fearful" situation we move from the intellectual part of our brain to the primitive part of our brain. This causes us to revert back to behavior that has helped us before and reuse the patterns we have stored. On average it takes us 11 times to create a new pattern and learn a new behavior. Eleven!

In addition to this we then create emotions to certain things, be it anger, happiness, frustration, or excitement, and these emotions trigger another part of our brain and link to the pattern in our brains all the more.

When we are excited by change, the new car, the new house, the new job and so on, the change in our emotions tells us everything is going to be OK and we find the change much easier to manage.

When we fear the change or feel sad about it, the chemical triggers from these emotions tell us we are in danger and we want to hold onto the patterns and behaviors we have always held onto; it's our fight-or-flight response that is there to keep us safe, but often it gets it wrong.

On top of this, if we are resisting the change because we are happy with things how they are, our childlike behaviors kick in and our internal five-year-old kicks in, and despite our best efforts to change (we know we need to, in order to keep our job, our relationship, and so on), sometimes we just can't muster up the change and then beat ourselves up even more.

To accept and deal comfortably with change we need to manage our emotions, and I know, this can be easier said than done. But, we are each capable of managing and changing our emotions, our beliefs, and our actions.

How did you feel when you got out of bed this morning? Did you think it was going to be a good day or a bad day? I bet whatever you thought is how your day turned out.

You wake up, say it's going to be a bad day, shower, and head down-stairs for breakfast. You spill your coffee, need to change only to find the top you just took out of the wardrobe also has a stain on it (darn coffee!). You run downstairs as you are now going to be late and the dog still needs walking. You leave the house, without the required poo bags, the dog doesn't want to do his business and is making you even more late, you finally get home, can't find your keys and run around frantically and then remember you put them in your back pocket when you took the dog out. You finally get in the car, the traffic is a nightmare, and you arrive late for the 9:00 a.m. meeting with everyone staring at you and you know it's because they have noticed yet another stain on your top.

Now let's look at the same morning, but you woke up feeling positive and said it was going to be a good day. You shower and dress, head downstairs, drink your coffee as you read your magazine, grab the leash and the poo bags, and take the dog for a walk as you notice the birds singing. You get home, grab your bag and your keys, jump in the car and your favorite song comes on the radio, the roads are clear, and you arrive in time to say hi to your team and grab a coffee before your 9:00 a.m. meeting.

The only difference to these situations is your mindset and your perception of how things are. If you can practice daily making choices first thing in the morning, when you find yourself faced with change you will be able to cope, embrace, and not only manage it but help lead it much more effectively.

Give it a go and see if you can create a smooth and comfortable change.

Top Tips for Embracing Change

- Pay attention to your emotions and your trigger points
- Remember that change is constant
- Know and accept that change can be tough, but it can also be great.

Mindset Not Process

When working with "businesses," I hear all too often that processes or systems are broken and that these need to be fixed to allow the organization to succeed.

Let's start by going backward here before we can move forward.

Businesses are people. I work with people at a business, not the business itself. Business coaches do not coach businesses, they coach people!

Processes and systems are designed and operated by people. If the system or process is "broken," it is usually human error or someone trying to bypass a system or process because it isn't fit for purpose or doesn't service the user in the way it should.

You don't change processes, you change behaviors and mindset and that in turn changes the process, if it needs changing.

I have sat in many meetings over the years and on many project teams when highly paid, professional consultants work with the "business" to fix or change a process.

During the meetings or projects I have looked at things from a people perspective, not a technology perspective or a financial perspective or a process perspective or any other perspective—but a people perspective.

- Why is something broken?
- What does the workforce need?
- How simple is it to use?
- What is the benefit to the end user?

Generally, the answer is, people aren't using it properly, or people aren't following the process.

Is that because it wasn't designed to meet their needs in the first place?

Remember mindset is based on beliefs. If we believe that that there is a work-around or a simpler way of doing things, processes and systems won't work because they weren't designed with people in mind.

Processes should be simple, straightforward, logical, and rational. If they miss any of these things they will break because our minds will find the most logical and rational route.

We also need to remember that our brain stores patterns. On average it takes us 11 times to learn something new. Do we allow anyone 11 opportunities to learn?

Very rarely.

Often we follow the process of

- I do, you watch
- I do, you help
- You do, I help
- You do, I watch

And expect the learning process to be completed, but we fail to pay attention to the emotional attachment and the "what's in it for me?" part of the change, and because the individual/s can't see the emotional benefit, they don't buy into it.

Imagine you're put in charge of your company's biggest leadership training program. You do everything right: you conduct extensive discovery with your subject-matter experts, you spend weeks authoring the storyboard, your executive team signs off, and you deliver an amazing training experience.

Everything goes beautifully and everyone agrees the training was a huge success.

Your work is done.

But back in your office, while you bask in the glory of your success, a dreadful thing is happening inside the brains of your students.

The neural networks that your training inspired are beginning to dissolve, and as a result, your employees are quietly forgetting almost everything you presented.

How bad is the problem?

How much do people forget?

Remember that we lose 80 percent of what we learn if we don't implement it within six days.

Some people remember more or less, but in general, the situation is appalling, and it is the dirty secret of corporate training: No matter how much you invest in training and development, nearly everything you teach to your employees will be forgotten.

Indeed, although businesses spend more than 50 billion pounds a year on training, this investment is like pumping fuel into a car that has a hole in the tank.

All of your hard work simply drains away.

And it gets worse.

Given that employees forget most of what they learn, we should have no hope that our training will transfer back to the workplace.

After all, memory is a necessary condition for behavior change, and if your employees have forgotten the lessons of your leadership seminar, there is no reason to expect them to become more effective leaders back in the workplace.

So if we consider that it takes 11 times before we create a new pattern and within six days 80 percent of the learning will have been forgotten, do you really expect the introduction of a new process or system to be picked up in just one training session, especially when your people don't really see the need for the new process in the first place?

Unfortunately, yes, in most cases you do.

We need to change mindsets and behaviors and then invest in the proper training if we really expect a process to fix a problem.

But remember, the process is only as good as the people using it and if it isn't logical and rational and simple and straightforward, it won't work.

Top Tips

- Remember that the business is only as good as the people within it.
- Processes should be designed with the end user in mind and not around a system.
- Provide plenty of opportunity to learn, digest, and refresh the information needed for something new.

Dear Past, thank you for all the lessons.
Dear Future, I am ready!

Mindset and Communication

Communication is not about speaking what we think. Communication is about ensuring others hear what we mean—Simon Sinek

I received the above from a friend of mine yesterday after we had both delivered presentations at an event. We are both very used to presenting and we both received great feedback, yet some of the questions we were asked in the panel discussion afterward caused us both to question what we had said.

I was asked a question about something I hadn't said, and my friend was asked something by several people about the work she did, despite covering this explicitly in the presentation.

We each of us only had 15 minutes to present what were quite meaty topics and so could have added a lot more information. We had both heard and understood what the other had said as did the majority of the audience, but did our knowledge of each other and the work we each do cloud what we heard and allow us to read into what we thought the other meant?

Communication is one of those topics that fascinate me immensely. Throughout my career I have heard people say how great they are at communicating, yet after a few minutes in their presence you realize they are very good at talking but less so at listening to others and taking on board what is being said.

I have attended courses, seminars, and workshops on communication and have on occasion been shocked by the presenters who fail to listen to the audience or participants.

A number of clients have brought me into their businesses to "fix" a problem, and in most cases, when you get down into the detail the problem is being caused by the inability to listen to people and act on what they are saying.

Often, we get so fixated on what we already know that we switch off from what is being said and ensuring that we have been understood and that we have understood others.

One particular person that I know will always try and reframe what I and others say, "So what you are trying to say is…" or "What you really mean is…." This particular person is an expert in their field, yet everyone who knows them comments on the fact they don't listen.

Are you hearing what others mean or are you reframing it to fit how you think and what you believe?

Where could you improve your communication with others?

How often do you speak what you think rather than ensuring others hear what you mean?

Mindset and Relationships

Now I know that this topic could quite easily have gone into the "Out of Work" section, but as we are focusing largely on fostering a mindset for success, I felt it prudent to include it here.

As I've highlighted throughout the book so far, our interactions are an important part of us being able to create a positive mindset, and those we spend our time with will, if we let them, turn a positive mindset into a negative mindset very quickly.

I've mentioned energy angels and energy vampires and when it comes to people in these categories, mindset is key to not letting it impact your energy.

Throughout your career you will have relationships with any number of people, from customers, colleagues, managers, trainers, lecturers, coaches, recruiters, suppliers, and so on; in addition to this you have your family, friends, and wider network. All of these people will, in some way, have an impact on you.

And you have a choice as to the impact that they make.

Too often we judge people too quickly. I totally understand that we are not here to like everyone and have everyone like us, some people will clash instantly, some will gel instantly and some will grow on us. But the impact of all of these interactions on our energy and our mindset is our choice.

No doubt you will come across some people in and out of work that you would sooner cross the road to avoid, but, when you allow yourself to feel this way, it has a chemical and physical reaction in you that causes you stress. The feelings you carry—you can control them, and you can change them. And it's not about becoming close friends with the person you want to avoid, but you have a choice about how to tolerate them.

In one of my roles there was a member of the executive team who at first seemed really nice. She was knowledgeable, professional, and appeared to want to do things differently and engage with her team. After a short while, a very different picture was being created. While she remained knowledgeable and professional, she didn't want to do things differently, didn't want to engage with anyone, was only looking out for herself and would stab you in the back as soon as she looked at you. I began to dread going to meet with her as I knew how I would feel afterward.

And then I changed my mindset.

You see I had been giving her power over how I felt, and in reality, nobody can control how we feel, except ourselves. So I told myself I wanted to feel calm at the end of every meeting with her. And I continued to focus on feeling calm as I walked to her office, and while I sat with her, and after a while, every time I saw her or had to meet with her, I left feeling calm, because I had a choice. I was the only person in control of my thoughts and feelings, and I was going to reclaim my personal power into how I wanted to feel.

And because I was focused on feeling calm, my behavior changed when I was with her, and while we would never be best buddies, we started working together better. She would still stab me and most of her colleagues in the back as quickly as she could, but I remained calm and did what I needed to do to control my part of the interaction, instead of trying to get her to change her approach. I later found out from one of my clients that the same person used to work there and they all felt the same about her, a mindset shift would appear to be beneficial to her and anyone else she may work with in the future.

You see when it comes to relationships, too often we spend too much time and effort focusing on what we want other people to change about themselves, when in reality, we can change the relationships and our interactions by changing our mindset and looking at things from a different perspective.

A business acquaintance, who for a while became somewhat of a friend, whom I met not long into starting business, had always niggled me slightly in the way she would expect me and others to do things for her and promote her business and the work she was doing, and expect me to "coach" her or help her with problems each time we met, yet on the one occasion that I needed a bit of help, she said she would help, but didn't, and the next I heard from her was when she wanted another favor. It began to really frustrate me and I used to feel so agitated every time I saw an update about her or her business. She wasn't going to change, so I had to. I changed the way I looked at her and our relationship, and I no longer feel frustrated or agitated by her. I wish her luck.

Top Tips

- Consider how you can change your mindset to improve your interactions and relationships with others.
- Reframe negative feelings about other people into something positive.
- Consider how your energy can be uplifted quickly by spending more time with angels immediately after some time with a vampire.

Mindset and Meetings

Aah, meetings, meetings. If your diary looks anything like mine used to then I feel for you, I really do. Some days I would arrive in London for an eight o'clock meeting and be in meetings through to six in the evening, sometimes even later, and then would have to catch up on my e-mails and calls, travel home, and then try and switch off before bed ready to repeat the pattern again the next day.

I had come to accept that this was the norm, and that at some point I would get done all of the actions that kept coming from all of the meetings I was in every day, or that I would find time to delegate what I needed to delegate to members of my team so they could get done what needed to get done by the time it needed to be done.

And on days when I had back-to-back meetings, I would often sit and wonder why I was even in the meeting in the first place.

Yet, because I accepted it was part and parcel of my job, it continued. I remained exhausted, my team were working at full capacity, and still the meetings kept coming. And then there were the meetings that were taking place to discuss the meeting we had just had, or the meeting we were going to have. And then because everyone was constantly in meetings, people were booking meetings with me, just so they could have a five-minute chat with me. But they didn't book it for five minutes; they would book it for half an hour or an hour, and then try and fill the time talking about irrelevant things, just because they had the time to do it.

So I changed my mindset.

First I changed the way I thought about meetings. I vowed to take away at least three pieces of useful and relevant information, and I started to look at meetings as positive interactions with my colleagues, and I stopped getting annoyed by the sight of everyone in the room being on their cell phones. I wanted to feel motivated and inspired by the meetings I was attending, and if I didn't feel that way, I questioned why.

I questioned the purpose of the meeting and why my attendance was required.

And then I had a meeting with my PA and asked her for every meeting invite to have an accompanying agenda so that I knew the purpose of the meeting, if I was required for the entire meeting or at all, and whether a call, lunch, or coffee would be more appropriate for one-to-one meetings. Within a week, my meetings began to lessen. I had time to do the work I needed to do and was having more positive interactions with colleagues outside of meeting rooms.

Within a few months, meetings across my peer group were lessening. We had found a way to interact more effectively and more productively without all of us sitting bored in a meeting together.

Some meetings began to be scheduled only for 15 minutes at a time and we would stand for the entire time. Meetings did not start or finish late.

Top Tips

- Understand the purpose and outcomes for the meeting
- Manage your mindset to manage your expectations
- Consider offering effective alternatives to work together

Mindset and Management

The right mindset can have a significant impact on the way that managers manage their employees. If you are a manager, this one is specifically for you. And if you have a manager, which the majority of people do unless they run their own business, then you can manage your mindset, as we talked about in the Mindset and Relationships section. You'll also find a case study about how one of my clients was able to improve the relationship she had with her manager.

So, with management comes great responsibility and perhaps even more of a need for a growth and positive mindset. No longer are you only responsible for yourself at work, but for other people too.

I hope that, if you are a manager, you have all of the support you need in your organization to help you succeed; if not, then please find ways to get it.

And while it pains me to say this, not all managers should be managers. Just because you were the tops salesperson, or the highest achiever in the team, it doesn't mean you have the skills to manage people effectively. And if you are one of those people that shouldn't be in the role, or you only took the job because of the compensation and rewards to go with it, please rethink your position. Your promotion and the agreement of your manager to put you in that position have something to do with mindset.

Anyway, I digress.

Let's get back to mindset and management responsibility. Over the last 10 years or so, more and more organizations have been deleting layers of management and expecting existing managers to take on more and more responsibility and still perform to a high standard.

For many, this has added to increased levels of stress, disengaged staff, decreased performance, and an increased workload.

It's here that I will refer you back first to the chapter on Mindset and Not Enough Time Mindset. The seven steps in that chapter will help you better manage your time by understanding your purpose, implementing your strategy, knowing the tools and resources you have available, how to say no, how to manage your energy, and who you are accountable to.

So let's look at this in a little more detail.

In your role, you are accountable for yourself and your team, and you are accountable to your manager and possibly stakeholders and customers, each of whom may have different expectations of you, your role, and your team.

So when you know who you are accountable to and for, you need to start mapping out your strategy. This must be aligned to your purpose (maybe not your "life purpose" but at the very least the purpose of your role). What is your role designed and intended to do, and how can you ensure the purpose of the role is met?

Role profiles, job descriptions, and the like are rarely, although they should be, a true reflection of the role you do. You may have a particular skill set so you have taken on additional responsibility; the role may have changed since you started because of financial, structural, or customer need. So spend time with those you are accountable to and for, and identify the real purpose of your role and the expectations of you in the role.

Then create a strategy. If time is short, what can you realistically focus on to fulfill the purpose and requirements of the role? Over what period? What are the priorities? What goals and objectives do you have, or want to create, to help the success of your team?

Who do you have in your team to help you deliver your strategy? Do you have enough people? Do you need some additional support? Do you need to call on additional skills? Do you need additional finances? Is there something you can say no to due to limited time, budget, resources, or people?

How will you keep your energy level up, and that of your team, to ensure you deliver what you need to deliver? How will you ensure that you and your team take regular breaks, find time to talk to one another, and stay uplifted? How much time will you spend with each of your team members to talk to them, learn about them, help them grow and develop? How much personal responsibility can you give them? Are they willing and able to be held to account for their role in the team success? How will you keep your stakeholders and team up to date on progress, issues, and successes?

In the Out of Work section of the book I've included a chapter on stress, which of course could have been included here, as the two are very much interconnected, but as you will have already read in chapter 1, sleep and rest play an important part in managing our stress levels, and when you have more than just yourself to think about at work, how you take care of yourself out of work is equally if not more important, and the same is applicable for your team.

If you are constantly stressed, busy, tired, don't have enough time, not enough hours in the day, got to work late again, catching your tail coming back, struggling to get off the hamster wheel, you need to stop.

You need to take time out. To stop, reflect, recharge, review the seven areas of focus relating to purpose-driven time management, and you need to start to work methodically, logically, and rationally.

We all have busy days, but these can spiral out of control if we let them, and in order to make a change, we need to change our thinking. And to stop you being the manager who 80 percent of the team are trying to get away from, take control of your mindset, to help you grow and support your team so that you can create more of the happy hormones when you achieve success.

Top Tips

- Stop, think, implement, review
- Focus on the seven areas of managing with purpose
- Understand from everyone who you are accountable to (and for) and the requirements of your role so that you can manage with purpose

Mindset and Leadership

There continues to be debate about who is a leader and who is a manager; leaders don't always manage people, but managers often lead. Leaders are not always those at the top of an organization, but for the purposes of this book, we will say that leaders are those that shape, direct, and lead the organization. They are the ones that shape and set the strategy for the organization, that are responsible for the direction of the business, setting the tone for the culture, and creating an environment to foster relationships and successful and enjoyable careers for all employees.

Leaders are likely, or should be, those that are looked up to as leading from the front, championing the way things get done in your organization, and being ambassadors for your brand and your company.

In addition to the techniques and areas of focus I discussed in the Mindset and Management chapter, leaders particularly need to manage their mindset in order to foster and maintain a successful career, set the culture of the organization, and lead, motivate, and engage staff at all levels.

As discussed in the Masculine and Feminine Mindset chapter, the way in which we lead our people is changing; our people want change and we need to change our approach to leadership.

A few years ago my coach was facilitating a large workshop in London, one of two annual events that she held in the UK away from her home in California. She told us how the week before she had been a panel member at an event talking about leadership with some of the most respected in the United States and the panel had been asked what they felt was the most important aspect of leadership. The most successful, respected, and admired leader from the panel simply answered "love."

She told us how she sat stunned. Never had she expected a male leader to make this comment, and certainly not one of the most renowned leaders at the event.

Leadership models talk more about compassion, authenticity, integrity, emotions, support, nurturing talent, and so on. Twenty years ago when I started work, while these may have been things I would have loved to see in my leaders in the same way that I had in my favorite teachers, these traits were certainly not things we were talking about in the workplace. In addition to these, we expect to work with autonomy, be responsible for our learning and development, have honest, open, and transparent conversations (HOT conversations as we call them at Chrysalis Consulting), and work for companies that have a social responsibility and create a positive impact in the world.

The *do as I say not as I do* type leadership, the command and control, the cracking of the whip, the promise of more and more money, is no longer what people and leaders need to change the way they act, interact, and speak—and they need to change their mindset.

The leaders that are not able to change are becoming extinct. Employees are calling them out, requesting change, and leaving when the values of the organization are not aligned to their own.

Leaders need to lead by keeping the vision and values of the organization alive and ensuring that the strategic direction of the business is aligned to these, while speaking honestly and openly with staff, valuing the people at all levels, being visible, engaging, and motivating, keeping stakeholders and customers happy, putting people first, showing compassion, integrity, authenticity, and, as it seems, love.

Leaders need to be able to tell stories instead of purely delivering statistics and KPIs. They need to set the tone for the organization, treat their people as able adults, and be able to manage the ever-changing financial and political landscape. Leaders need to be one step ahead of the game and need to encourage innovation and creativity.

And this may all just be the beginning.

Leaders need a positive mindset, a growth mindset, a mindset for success, and an entrepreneurial, purpose-driven, and value-driven mindset. They need to be able to show emotions and keep the energy high. They need to focus, set strategy, say no, and speak and act with authority and compassion.

I speak to many leaders who owe their success and their vision and insight to meditation and/or mindfulness. I have covered this in greater detail later in the book, but if leaders are seeing this as a key to their success, then it might be something you want to consider. Nancy Kline's book *Time to Think* is one I recommend regularly to clients and friends. The concept that we each need thinking time every day in order to help us grow is a key point. Leaders, managers, and employees at all levels, even when at home, should create time in our day for thinking, growing, and managing our mindset.

Leaders are now more visible than ever, and it takes broad shoulders and the right mindset to foster a career as a successful leader.

Top Tips

- Be your authentic self
- Develop emotional intelligence as your key skill
- Manage your energy in order to effectively manage your mindset and lead your organization successfully

Mindset and Procrastination

I don't know anyone who hasn't at some point in their life, or at several points during the day, put things off that they should be doing either to focus on something else, or because the task seems too big or they don't know where to start.

Over the years, and with every one of my clients that I have spoken to, as well as really identifying when and why people procrastinate, the one thing that comes up regularly is fear.

Sometimes this is a fear that the task is too big and overwhelming, sometimes it's fear of failure, and sometimes even a fear of success. But fear appears to be the biggest driver of procrastination.

As I look into this more, factors such as time have a part to play. But when we consciously put things off, or find ourselves distracted by e-mails, phone calls, social media, cups of coffee, and such, fear is the number one factor for procrastination.

This can be putting off tasks, conversations, projects, activities, change, even exercise, or a healthy living regime.

As I've highlighted earlier in the book, fear drives a certain chemical response in us, and this can have implications on doing anything that is likely to drive a shift or a change.

I've also learned that fear steps up when ego takes over and our inner voice pipes up telling us that we can't do something.

Ego is our inner protection, and I've found that ego drives our fear, especially when we are stepping up and out of our comfort zone. More about ego in the next section.

Procrastination can of course slow us down, hinder our development, hinder our career progression, hold us back in relationships, impact our time management, and much, much more.

So is there a cure?

I've found two ways of overcoming procrastination that have helped me and everyone I have shared them with.

First, when you find yourself putting something off, stop and ask yourself why. What's the answer?

Second, set a timer or watch the clock, and give yourself 15 minutes of doing whatever it is you are procrastinating. Just 15 minutes. We can all focus for that amount of time. Give it a go, and see if you notice a difference.

I've found, and so has everyone that I have shared this with, that after 15 minutes, the feeling of not wanting to do the task has gone, any fear or negative thoughts have disappeared, and one is able to keep going, moving forward, and getting on with the task in hand.

Fifteen minutes, what have you got to lose?

PART III

Out of Work Mindset

I've mentioned throughout the book that life balance is what we should be seeking, and I don't believe that everything fits neatly into a box at work and out of work. We are whole people and everything that happens in our lives is interconnected with and impacts other areas of our lives. But some things are more likely to be things that happen out of work, but that can impact us at work, and so I've split them up for the purposes of this book. There will be parts of your life that aren't covered in any section of this book, but the principles will be the same.

Find what works for you when it comes to fostering a mindset for a successful career.

Alcohol and Mindset

Drinking was always a social activity. Meeting friends at the pub on an evening or weekend, walking the dog to the pub with my partner, pay-day drinks with the team, networking over wine or champagne, a glass (bottle) of wine after a stressful day at work or when celebrating success.

Then there were the parties, the dinners, the award evenings, and the lunches where wine was being brought to the table on tap. Alcohol was everywhere in my life and played a major part in work and social activities.

I was always quite a big drinker (although I rarely drank at home), enjoyed a cocktail or two while out with friends, could get through a lot of vodka, but as I got older my tolerance to alcohol decreased and the hangovers began to last three days. A three-day hangover after a team night out is not an effective or productive way of growing a career.

Each time I was curled up on the sofa declaring that I would never drink again, I meant it.

Until the next time I went out.

I would never have a good night's sleep when I had been out drinking, even after a couple of glasses, so I always felt exhausted the next day, but as everyone around me felt the same, it didn't seem to be a big deal. It was something we were all getting used to, the three-day hangover becoming a bit of a joke and all of us confirming that we could no more party as hard as we could when we were younger.

I had to stop drinking when I started my medication to prevent me from having seizures, and while I thought I would miss it, I didn't. I could go out, last the evening, hold my own in conversations, dance the night away, and not wake up feeling awful the next day. I was sleeping better, feeling better, had more energy, and was losing weight as the binge eating or reaching for junk food wasn't happening.

Even now, though I have stopped taking my medication I haven't started drinking again. I did have three lagers after work one Friday, but regretted it as soon as I got home and I haven't started again since. I'm not declaring myself as someone who will never drink again, but for now, I'm happy not doing it.

My partner and I were walking through our local shopping center one lunchtime when we bumped into a friend. He had been a big drinker, and I mean a big drinker, and looked so much slimmer and healthier. He told us he hadn't drunk for months and was feeling so much better. He told us he had realized that drinking was making him feel low and anxious and almost depressed the morning after, and he stopped drinking for a month. He went out when the month was up, felt awful again the morning after, and hasn't touched a drop since.

Now I'm not saying that everyone needs to stop drinking, I used to enjoy it and I know many, many people who still do. But for me, and our friend, the lows after the highs just weren't worth it anymore.

I used to feel so anxious the next day, wondering if I had upset anyone, said the wrong thing, embarrassed myself, become even louder than normal, or done or said something I would later regret. Now if I do any of those things it's not because of the drink.

I also knew that at stressful times I would escape by going for a drink with friends or family to help me switch off. I wasn't really switching off though, as the stress was exacerbated the following day making me feel more anxious and more stressed, and on occasion reaching for the bottle again. Luckily, I only drank at weekends and sometimes not for weeks, but rarely would one drink ever be just one. There was always a reason for just one more, and then when I was ready to head home it would be *one for the road*.

While studying psychotherapy, I learned a lot about the effect of alcohol on our brains, and why our sleep patterns and thoughts can change while drinking, and this has given me different view. BUT, though now I am a "nondrinker," I don't push my view onto others.

If you want to foster a mindset for career success, consider your daily and weekly alcohol intake. Monitor your sleep patterns when you've had and haven't had a drink and see if you can identify a difference. After a drink, see how you feel the following morning. Do you feel refreshed and ready for the day ahead? Or would you rather have a duvet day at home.

(I've also stopped drinking tea and coffee as well as I didn't like how they were making me feel, so now I just drink water, fruit juices, and peppermint tea—ever the party girl!)

Mindset Tips

- If alcohol is a "relaxant" for you, find another way to reduce stress and anxiety.
- Drink in moderation.
- Don't let alcohol dictate how much you enjoy yourself on a night out.
- Don't judge those that don't drink—or constantly keep trying to push drinks onto them.
- Respect the beliefs of those around you.

The difference between who you are and who you want to be is how you think.

Mindset and Medication

I'm not one for dosing myself up on medication and pumping chemicals into my body and I believe the best way to sustain a healthy body and a healthy mind is through a balanced diet and exercise.

In June 2015 I started having blackouts and dizzy spells. I had suffered from petit mal epilepsy as a young teenager and while these spells felt somewhat the same, the aftereffects were significantly different and I found myself feeling totally exhausted after an episode.

I visited my doctor and, to cut a long story short, was told not to drive and referred to a specialist.

On September 10 (my birthday) at 5.15 a.m., I visited a neurologist and was immediately booked in for an MRI and EEG.

In October I was prescribed medication for epilepsy to stop the seizures. The dosage was quite high and would double in two weeks; the doctor told me it may take some time to get used to, he wasn't wrong.

During the first two weeks on the pills, I felt light, everything was funny, and I mean everything, and it was bit like being drunk for two weeks. One particular Friday while in the office, I could only be thankful that I had no clients to see that day as I doubt they would have come back. I couldn't walk in a straight line, and my head was getting fuzzier and fuzzier as though I had consumed a lot of alcohol for breakfast and topped it up at lunch. I was in a hysterical mood and could not control my laughing. I left the office early, came home, and slept.

A few days later I was on a double dose of medication and within just a couple of days the effects were awful. I felt low, lethargic, and struggled to get out of bed in the mornings or off the sofa during the day.

Walking the dog started to feel like a chore, and each day I was becoming slower and more lethargic. I rang the consultant who informed me that depression was a common side effect of the medication and offered to prescribe some antidepressant medication. I kindly refused.

I did not want to pump myself with one pill to make me low and another to level me out, no way!

Part of me wished I had, though, as over the next two weeks I would spend hours every night crying. Crying over everything, what was on TV, what wasn't on TV, my weight, dinner, tiredness—you name it I cried over it—I was becoming uncontrollable, my emotions were becoming uncontrollable, yet despite all of the crying and emotion, I was able to have rational conversations with my partner and family.

I told them I didn't know why I was crying but that surely it was a reaction to the medication and that I just needed to get used to what was happening until it eased off.

I was rationally and logically telling them that I was working from the primitive part of my brain, which was due to a change in the chemical balance, and that I would be OK soon. The crying continued, and I accepted it would get better and that, while I was so emotional, I just needed time and to keep thinking and acting as logically and rationally as I could.

The crying lasted two weeks, hours every night, and as the crying stopped my mood worsened and my interactions became less.

I didn't want to leave the house, I struggled to drag myself out of bed every day just to get to the office, my work was suffering as the thought of speaking to anyone or meeting with anyone was too much to bear, but I took each day as it came. Did what I needed to do, went home, and slept.

That was my life for weeks, but I continued thinking it was a temporary side effect and that things would subside. I just needed to get myself back into the logical and rational part of my brain and everything would be OK.

A week before Christmas I hit rock bottom. I hadn't been functioning properly for months and was unable to drive; my mood was impacting me, my partner, and the business; money was beyond tight; and to top it off, what little we did have had been lost when my card was cloned. I had no idea how we would get through Christmas, pay our team, or have a Christmas dinner.

Still I kept telling myself that things would improve and I just needed to start acting, thinking, and interacting positively, but it was exhausting.

Christmas Eve came and all I could think about was whether I would be better jumping off the bridge onto the train track or jumping in the river; it kept going round and round and round in my head.

The logical part of my brain knew I wouldn't actually take my life, and gave a number of really good reasons.

First, to jump off the bridge onto the track I would need to climb up onto the side and given my current weight and lack of strength I wouldn't get up there. The only way that was going to happen would be if I took a stepladder and if people saw me carrying and then climbing onto a ladder they would surely stop me, so that wasn't an option.

Second, to jump into the river, which is not very deep, I would need to walk a few miles up. I would need to wear really heavy clothes and possibly put stones in my pocket, and in all the times I had walked past the river I hadn't seen anything small enough to fit in my pocket and heavy enough to pull me down into the water.

So, I wasn't going to do anything today.

But I couldn't get the thoughts out of my head and it started to panic me. I spoke to my partner about what was going on in my head and asked him to talk it through with me. If I couldn't get my mind on something else I feared he would have to have me admitted to hospital.

We talked it through, everything that was going in my head, and agreed I wasn't going to do anything today because I had no rocks and would look silly with a ladder.

We agreed I wouldn't do anything the next day because it was Christmas and I didn't want him or my family or friends to have to deal with that, and we agreed that Boxing Day wasn't a good idea either because it was too close to Christmas.

We then sat and watched a film and I fell asleep. When I woke it was time to take my second pill of the day; I couldn't do it.

Knowing how low I had fallen that day I had to get myself back on track; I needed to be logical, rational, and positive; I couldn't take another pill. And I didn't.

Within three days I was getting back to my normal self and I haven't gone back on the medication. I'm managing my condition myself through diet, mindfulness, and mindset exercises.

Had I not understood why I was feeling the way I was, I don't know if I would be here now.

Medication, whether you're self-medicating or taking prescription meds, can impact your energy, your motivation, your mindset, and ultimately your life.

There will be times when medication is needed to keep you alive, and please do not stop taking something that you need, but try and identify alternatives, working with your medical professional if you can, to help you create a healthy body and a healthy mind.

Top Tips

- Seek alternative natural ways to medicate and heal yourself
- Understand your own thought and behavioral patterns
- Know what is best for you in terms of your health

When you feel like quitting think about why you started

Mindset and Psychotherapy/Hypnotherapy

I had been coaching for years but I felt I could be offering and providing something more for my coaching clients to help them see and feel results much more quickly and at a deeper level.

I was amazed at just how many of my clients in senior positions would apologize for ever talking about anything personal or anything out of work.

We shouldn't apologize for our lives, we are a whole person and while at times we can feel as though we only need to focus on one particular area, whether we like it or not, work can impact life and life can impact work. We don't have an off switch when we walk into or out of the office and if we try too hard to disconnect, largely we are the ones to suffer.

I started seeking something additional that I could incorporate into my coaching, something to help my clients more. I did some research and most of the coaches and companies I found used NLP (neuro-linguistic programming) as an additional tool. For one reason or another I had never been a huge fan of pure NLP and I kept looking.

I came across a hypnotherapy qualification and I started to look at this path more. I found a qualification in my town that focused more on neuroscience and why we feel the way we do, and the qualification was as a clinical hypnotherapist and psychotherapist. This was it, the missing piece of the puzzle. I made inquiries and met with the lecturer a couple of weeks later.

We discussed how I wanted to use this and he agreed this would be a great addition and provide some additional tools in the toolbox, and I started the course.

I had already completed my psychology degree and had been reading and researching behaviors and mindset for years, and this was indeed the missing piece of the puzzle.

I started to combine everything I was learning into my coaching practice and was totally blown away by just how quickly my clients were moving forward.

I worked with two executives as part of my case studies, both of whom were displaying visible signs of stress. By the end of the first session both mentioned how light and positive they felt.

Within just a couple of sessions it was like I was looking at different people. Their appearance, their mood, the way they were talking totally transformed; it was like magic.

The tools I was learning as part of this qualification were solution focused as I had learned in my coaching, but started with the question, "What's been good?"

Not "How do you feel?" or "How are you?" but "What's been good?" This immediate shift makes us focus on the positives and from here the session continues.

I've been able to expand on my knowledge of the 3 Ps: Positive Actions, Positive Interactions, and Positive Thoughts, and by focusing on these areas clients are able to transform all areas of their lives.

By focusing on the positives we are automatically working in the intellectual part of our brain and move away from the primitive part of our brain. This allows us to think logically and rationally and make the best decisions and also sparks creativity.

Hypnotherapy and psychotherapy are fast becoming the leading therapies in the UK and a lot of research is being undertaken by leading schools and therapists to demonstrate the advantages.

In a nutshell, by focusing on the positives we start to think positively and because the brain doesn't know the difference between reality and imagination we start to have the release of the happy chemicals which then start to make us feel better.

Hypnotherapy and psychotherapy, specifically when used in a solution-focused way, trigger the right chemicals that in turn reduce feelings of stress and anxiety and make us happier in all areas of our lives.

Top Tips

- Focus on what's been good
- Find ways to think, act, and interact positively
- Find ways to release happy chemicals
- Use relaxation as a way to empty your stress bucket and eliminate signs and feelings of stress and anxiety

Parenting and Mindset

Growing up I always knew I would have a family and as a teen I decided I would have kids when I was 35. When I was 11 or 12, I found out that twins were in the family and having skipped a generation, my cousins, my brother or sister, or I were likely to have twins. I decided it would be me, and unexpectedly, aged just 19, fell pregnant with my twin sons and gave birth to them three months after my 20th birthday.

The boys' dad and I got together when we were 17 and had a very emotional relationship. We were constantly hot and cold, on and off and when I found out I was pregnant we had just started another "off" phase.

I was working for a large retailer and had just completed my management training and secured a nice pay rise and was preparing to move onto the next level of my training and into my chosen specialism of Training.

I was 19, single, newly promoted, and had just moved back in with my parents to help me save some money, but I knew having the boys would be the right decision and that I would do it on my own if I needed to.

For the next six months I stayed at home with my parents and the twins' dad stayed with his dad; we started to save, I continued to work, and then due to some complications and extremely high blood pressure I was signed off work. This wasn't helped by the store manager who had twin girls, put me on the early morning shift and told me that pregnancy was easy and a total breeze and to just get on with it. I didn't return until my sons were four months old.

Throughout my pregnancy I feared not being a good enough mum, not being able to give them everything they needed and worried about what would happen if I didn't bond with them or didn't love them. I would panic during the day because there was little movement, only to be kept awake at night by feet kicking into my rib cage, bladder, and kidneys.

I felt amazed each time I went for a scan and saw them, every time I heard their heartbeats, and every time I had a bath as the water rippled by the arms, legs, and feet that would kick me from the inside.

The twins were born in 2000, one week before Christmas, and when they were born I was ill. I stayed in hospital for a week, and decided I would not be in hospital for Christmas, so on Christmas Eve I got showered, got dressed, and put on some makeup. I was sitting in the chair when the doctors came round, I told them I felt amazing; they told me I looked it and I was discharged, on the promise that my midwife would check my blood pressure at home every day until their concerns went away.

I didn't want to be seen a failure, I wanted to be the best mum I could be. When the health visitors came to the house the house was clean, the washing in, bottles prepared, and children asleep. Everyone thought I was superwoman and I kept pushing so as not to disappoint.

When my sons were just four months old, having been forced to take maternity leave early, I returned to work and my sons went to a childminder. I would drop them off in the morning, be at work 10 minutes early, work hard, push for my next promotion, pick the boys up on my way home, cook dinner, clean, wash clothes, sort bottles, pack bags for the next day, sort the boys' baths and settle them to bed with a story before exercising and going to bed.

The routine lasted for as long as I had energy for, and then the housework started to slip. Asking the kids' dad for help (we were on an "on" phase) was falling on deaf ears—after all he had "worked all day," like I hadn't, and quickly I started to spiral. I felt the world was against me and I looked for happiness in shoes, handbags, household items, nights out with my friends, and wine. Life was good and I was fine (not).

To the outside world everything was rosy, except to my parents who noticed I was going out far too often. I felt I had lost my sense of identity, had no idea who I was, wouldn't sleep properly (for years), but kept on going, feeling broken on the inside but a shining example of superwoman on the outside. When I left one employer, the marketing team even made me a card with "Kelly Fryer: Superwoman" on it and my head placed on her body.

When my sons were five and I felt I had hit rock bottom I went to see a doctor as I couldn't cope any longer. They prescribed pills, I refused to take them. I started exercising, drinking less, and journaling. I got a new job and gained seven promotions in eight years, worked long hours as the main breadwinner in the house; my then husband (we were on an "on" phase and married) was helping so much in the house and life was good, great even. I was truly balancing home and work and I was succeeding.

In 2013, I realized I could start my own business (three months later it was started). I had no savings, no Plan B, no clients as yet, and only three months' money to see me through. I started working with professionals as a coach, and with large businesses on Change and HR. I was planning my own diary, spending more time with my sons than I probably had in all their life; I was happy, even though I had less money.

I jumped from corporate because I knew I could do a better job than some of the coaches my employer was working with and I knew I could make a difference to the people I wanted to work with.

I'm a great mum, with two polite, strong-minded, intelligent sons, and even though at times they are grunting teenagers, I am a lucky mum. I deliver talks on the fact that superwoman isn't a working mum (I mean really, you can't shop in that outfit), I support professional women balance work and life, I have overcome "mummy guilt," and I do the absolute best I can.

Our kids want time and attention, and as long as we give them as much of that as we can and believe we are the best mum in the world, then we are.

Top Tips

- There is no parenting rule book, just be the best you can be.
- Remember: Superwoman isn't a working mum—and who wants that outfit anyway!
- Don't try and do it all—if all else fails get a cleaner, I'm so grateful for mine.

Mindset, Rest, and Relaxation

Taking some time out for some R&R?

Chances are, if you are anything like me it will be more relaxation and less rest, though until recently I thought they were the same thing.

So I *do* things to relax:

- Listen to music
- Yoga
- Cycle
- Drink (only occasionally now)
- See friends
- Go for dinner
- Read
- Write
- Learn
- Cook
- Clean
- Watch a film
- Take a walk
- Play board games
- Go out with my sons
- Journaling

I Do Stuff!

Anything other than work really helps me relax. But when you love what you do, it's not really work, so sometimes I work to relax.

And it helps me relax, but *doing* is not resting.

I found this a real shock, like a real shock. People were actually telling me to do nothing, and I'm not the sort of person to just do nothing. I mean nothing!! Who does that?

It turns out quite a lot of people, and it's good for you. Of course I knew that, but I have never been able to do nothing.

For years my Mum has tried to encourage me to rest. So I did, and I rested by doing stuff. My Oracle cards tell me to rest, so I do stuff. My body and my mind say rest, so I do stuff, all the while telling myself that relaxation and rest are the same thing.

Until I put into practice some of my learning for myself. A simple mindset shift, I told myself that I wasn't doing nothing, I was resting. And just like that, it worked. I say just like that, it was when I actually listened to the messages I was being given that it worked, I had ignored these messages for 35 years.

I went to Rebecca Campbell's London event a few months ago with one of my amazing friends Lindsay. Rebecca stood on stage and told a story of when she lay on the floor watching a spider for an hour.

What?

Who does that, lying on the floor watching a spider! Yes, of course, it's fine for you isn't it, best-selling author with hundreds of clients having time to rest; what about the rest of us?

And you mean resting is really just that, resting and doing nothing.

Not reading, writing, listening to music, watching a film, yoga, walking, spending time with friends, and so on. It really is just doing nothing.

Yep, I can't do that, how will I ever get anything done?

Still they kept coming. Everyone I spoke to, every time I meditated, I kept getting the same message about resting. I would promise to do more yoga and keep trying mindfulness—that way I'm resting while doing something.

Still the messages kept coming.

How can I possibly rest with so much to do? I'm building a business and a charity, and another business, and I run a home and I'm a mum, a partner, a daughter and a sister, and a friend. And I want to write and learn and be a success and earn money and pay for holidays and a new car and arrange a party and get the shopping done and exercise and train for a half-marathon, and everything else that needs doing.

I'm not a success like Rebecca Campbell. It's fine for her to lie on the floor watching spiders for an hour but I can't do that. And it's fine for my Mum to ask me to rest, she's never really done it for herself but she wants me to do it. People just don't get me and I don't have time to rest.

A post then came up on my Facebook feed for a 15-minute chat and an energy clearing for free. That's what I needed.

I messaged Louise, the lady who had made the post, said yes please, and we arranged to talk on Wednesday.

On the Monday before the call I started to use my new planner to plan my day, even scheduling in yoga, meditation, and mindfulness. My day was full from six in the morning till nine in the evening. I was going to be amazing with such a jam-packed and awesome plan!

On Wednesday I had the call with Louise. I explained my blocks. She told me I would never be a true success and achieve all I wanted to achieve if I didn't rest.

Louise told me to rest. She said she would be doing the clearing soon and we would talk in one week, but to be a magnet for my clients I would have to rest.

Who wants to be a magnet anyway, I do not have time to rest.

By the end of the 30-minute call I had promised I would rest. I ended the call and went straight back to work, but found myself stopping before I sat down in front of my computer.

I checked my diary, scheduled the Friday and the following Tuesday off work as I had no clients on those days (I was booked for all of August anyway), made some lunch, and sat for the afternoon. Yes I had work to do, but nothing that couldn't wait. I couldn't believe I was saying all of this to myself.

An hour later Louise messaged me to say she had done the clearing, she felt it needed to be done quickly and I told her about all of the time off I had booked and that I was currently just sitting looking out of the window, resting.

I felt a bit emotional the following day (the clearing, possibly) and told my other half and business partner about me needing rest. We agreed on two weeks off in August instead of the entire month, and I booked two weeks away in October and lots of days off.

I meditated for an hour on Thursday morning before reading and writing in the evening after work. I promised I would rest more before bed.

Then on Friday, I tried the "rest thing" again, planning to do it for the day. I couldn't get comfortable. I was fidgeting, moving, standing up and walking about, getting glasses of water, and then needing to go to the restroom. I thought I would just check my e-mails and found myself stopping, went to turn on the TV and stopped and then at 10:20 a.m. I found a spot on the sofa, covered myself up with a blanket, opened up my heart chakra, and other than a couple of very quick toilet breaks and two additional glasses of water, I lay there for five hours.

Yep, five hours.

I breathed, I received, I relaxed, and I was grounded. I went inside myself clearing blocks and pain. I unraveled my solar plexus for what felt like hours as though it were a ball of bandages. Peeling back layer upon layer of bandage, the past and protection. All the hurt, all the rejection, all the loss, all the emotion, unraveling and unraveling and unraveling, on and on it went.

When I was "complete" my other half rang to say we had a client lead that involved lots of money and every day since then a new opportunity has presented itself.

On the Tuesday I tried again for a mammoth resting session, after just 40 minutes I felt ready to get on with the day. I had done the hard work, now was daily and weekly resting.

Rest is good. Rest is needed. Rest allows you time to think and create, and get creative and innovate. Rest creates room for yes. I need daily rest now, and I create the time for it. Sometimes it's a set time each day and some days just when needed. Sometimes it's an hour, sometimes two, sometimes only 15 minutes.

Time to rest. Time to relax. Time to meditate. Time to show up. Time to grow.

When we are constantly on the hamster wheel and running, becoming consumed by all that is happening around us, this stops us being creative.

Ever found yourself getting into bed at night and your head is filled with ideas, thoughts from the day, all the things you need to do tomorrow or should have done today?

Ever found that you have your best ideas in the shower first thing in the morning or find a solution to a problem that you have been racking your brain on for months?

This happens when you allow yourself time to think.

It's not the ideal time of the day to be having your genius moments, but it's probably the only time of the day where you have stopped and allowed your mind to process everything it needs to, and the first time you have allowed yourself an opportunity to hear the ideas in your head.

Top Tips

- Find ways to relax doing things you enjoy.
- Create time in your day to rest—don't wait to find time, it will be like looking for a needle in a haystack.
- Find time during the day just to listen to and jot down your thoughts—this will improve your sleep and your creativity.

Mindset and Ego

Oh, ego, ego, ego!

Sometimes very helpful, she/he helps you stay driven and determined and then when you are getting a little bit too big for your boots she/he shoots you down. Just last month I was writing in my journal. I had a particular question that I had been asking for guidance on and this voice kept shouting in my head with an answer, but it didn't feel right.

"Is this ego giving the answer?"

"Yes."

"Is it the right thing for me to do?"

"No."

"Then why suggest it?"

"We didn't, ego did."

Helpful? Yes. I knew on that occasion something didn't *feel* right and I went with my gut instead. I then spent all day thinking about ego. I've done the research, and I know that the voice of self-limiting belief is only there to protect me and that it comes from fear or other emotional patterns in our brain.

But could I realistically stop it?

I had tried techniques before, thanking ego for keeping me safe and telling her/him to go now, but she/he still stayed in my head, I could still hear her/him shouting.

I tried talking to her/him, she/he of course told me I was stupid. Not what I wanted to hear. Later that day as I went to journal again, I sat down with *Raise Your Vibration* by Kyle Gray; it's the first book where I've actually followed one tip a day instead of plowing through the entire book. Today's vibe was about ego! I read the vibe, finished my journaling, and then picked up off the bookshelf *A course in Miracles Made Easy* by Alan Cohen, which is all about ego.

Both authors suggest making friends with the pesky voice. Not telling it to shut up, or to leave, but for now just to give you a break and come back when you've got something juicy for it to focus on. It works and it's amazing.

Let's try and put this into context. I'm getting ready to go out, to see a client, shopping, night out, it doesn't matter where, just out. I've decided what I want to wear, I put it on, and there she/he comes. "You're not seriously going to wear that, are you?" And gives me ten thousand reasons why I shouldn't.

I can of course listen, change my outfit ten thousand times and go back to outfit number one, or I can tell my ego, "Thanks for showing up, you are always here when I need you. I'm getting ready right now, but feel free to come back just as I'm about to walk into wherever I'm going." And she/he does.

So I'm walking into a speaking gig/client meeting/shop/restaurant/ bar, and ego comes back. "You're not seriously going in there are you? like that? Who do you think you are? Who do you think you are to think you can do this? They won't like you, they won't listen, they will take one look at you and switch off." But this time I need ego. I need ego right now and she/he came back right on cue. I don't need all of this negative talk, but I do need her/him.

> Thanks, ego, for showing up, right on cue. You are always here whenever I need you. I don't need this negativity right now, but I do need you to help this. We are going to go in there and we are going to strut our stuff, and talk our talk and walk our walk, and we are going to shine, and you are going to help me and make sure that I'm being the best me and doing what I need to do.

And ego's off. She/he has got a new job, the one to tell you how amazing and talented and knowledgeable and perfect you are just the way you are, she/he becomes your best friend instead of your worst enemy and it works.

You strut, you shine, you soar and you don't hear from her/him for the rest of the day.

Sometimes she/he works the opposite, though. You tell yourself that you can't leave looking like that, feeling awful and lacking confidence in every outfit that you try on. And in she/he comes, telling you how amazing you are, helping you choose an outfit and kicking you out of the door. Ego is the one that pushes you into interviews. Sends you to the restroom before a big meeting to give yourself a pep talk in the mirror. And, ego's there to help you when you move off track. I had this recently. I was about to give a talk to my biggest ever audience and was asked to arrive early for a sound check. As I did, I saw the empty seats all of them, there were loads. The fact they were empty didn't faze me, but the fact they would soon be full did. Oh my god!!

I'm usually excited about speaking, but not today. New talk, different venue, and I was wearing flats. I've been wearing them a lot lately as they make me feel more grounded. I could not go on stage. What if they didn't like me? What if I messed up? What if this new talk was a load of rubbish? Arrgghh. Panic. I could say I was sick, that I'd lost my voice, that I'd been abducted by aliens, and I could vanish. Yes, that's it, I'll vanish.

We did the sound check, I needed air and then ego came. "Hi ego, thanks for showing up, right on cue, just when I need you." "Just who do you think you are?" she/he asks. "What makes you think this is all about you?" The people coming today have paid good money to listen to you and the organizers have gone to a lot of trouble. You are here today to teach these people something, and if you have to tell them how you nearly got abducted by aliens, just to show how "normal" you are, then do it. But you will not let these people down. You know exactly what you are talking about. And quite frankly, nobody gives a crap about your shoes.

That was me told then.

Often, ego is there to protect, to keep you safe and away from harm. But sometimes ego gets it wrong. Usually mine comes along when I'm stepping up. Stepping up is about going into the unknown, out of your comfort zone and into your true purpose. And it doesn't really matter which side of the fence ego is on at the time, as long as you get up and do it.

Learn to listen to your ego, understand when she/he comes and when she/he is trying to protect you and when she/he just wants to hold you back. If ego and intuition say no, something isn't right—don't do it. If intuition and ego say different things, always go with your gut. And if they both say yes, you probably aren't stretching far enough to fly.

Mindset and Stress

How Full Is Your Bucket?

"OMG I am so stressed."

Sound familiar?

I hear this so often, as people scurry around with not enough time, too much to do, and ever-changing demands. For many people stress is a reality, but do we overuse the word?

Stress impacts us all in different ways and a good amount of stress is actually good for us, it's what gets us out of bed in the mornings, allows us to reach deadlines and targets, plan events, and beat our previous personal best.

But what if it gets too much?

Unhealthy stress can have unhealthy effects on us. We can lose sleep, become irritated easily, eat too much of the wrong foods, worry about the smallest of things, and stop doing the things that ordinarily make us happy or give us energy.

Often, when we are operating in the unhealthy stress levels, this can pile up into a stress bucket. We go to bed worrying about things and wake up still worrying the next morning. When we are stressed we produce stress hormones and when we produce these it can impact our sleep. When we don't sleep properly we become more stressed, produce more stress hormones, find our stress bucket become more full or even overflowing, and find ourselves in a vicious cycle of being stressed, tired, and underperforming.

The days are becoming longer and more daylight certainly helps our state of mind but what can we do for ourselves to lift our mood, empty our stress buckets, and start to feel calmer and more relaxed?

Try one or a combination of the tips below and notice the shift in your stress levels.

- Take time out with a hot bath or lie down on the bed for 15 minutes

- Read a good book
- Go for a walk or do 30 minutes of exercise
- Treat yourself to a massage
- Switch off your phone and e-mails, even just for half an hour and ideally at least an hour before bed
- Take a couple of days away from social media
- Turn your music up in the car or dance around the house
- Drink more water
- Eat more fruit and vegetables
- Try meditation, relaxation, or mindfulness even if just for 10 minutes

Small, simple changes can make the world of difference to our mental and physical well-being.

And if you are looking at the list and filling it with lots of "ifs" and "buts" or have tried one or more of these before and it hasn't made a difference, download the free relaxation audio via my website www.chrysalis-consulting.co.uk.

Stress doesn't have to be a way of life or something you have to live with; you can reduce the stress in your bucket relatively quickly and get you back to living the life you want.

Try a small step today.

And Finally ...Getting Out of Your Own Way

At times, it feels like the world is against us, "busy" is all we seem to be yet little progress is made. We put things off until tomorrow, we find ourselves feeling less than those around us, and we doubt ourselves, our abilities, and our thoughts. And we get in our own way whether we realize it or not.

What if, just for one moment, you could close your eyes, take a nice couple of deep breaths, and see yourself in the life you want, in the career you want, doing what you want.

Did you see it? Great, what's next?

You start processing those thoughts and the ideal life, you see it, you feel it, but then reality kicks in. You see it but so many things are in the way; kids, work, money, time, and so on.

This life you imagine seems so close and yet so far. This life you can imagine, is surrounded by "ifs" and "buts."

"I could do that if......"

"Of course I want to do that but......"

You and only you will know what you are filling those blanks with and where those mental blocks are coming from. Only you will know where you are getting in your own way.

In this section I will share some of my techniques that, when considered and implemented with no "ifs or buts," can move you out of your own way.

Superwoman/man Wasn't a Working Parent—Comparison Syndrome

Social media is filled with slim, pretty, glamorous people from all walks of life. People share their successes, pictures of their pristine children, new cars, beautifully decorated homes, and images of nights out in fab locations with lots of happy smiling friends.

I work 50 or more hours a week, have four kids, a partner, exercise and daily practices to do, and a home to look after. All I want to do with any spare time is sit in my comfy clothes, watch brain-numbing TV, and have take-out. The chances of me posting pictures on social media?

Zero.

Partly because it takes effort to lift my phone, partly because posting a picture of me is likely to scare the web, but actually, it's me time and while on occasion I may post "comfy night in front of the TV with my boys" and get lots of likes and comments, I rarely do it.

Taking time out to recharge is my time. Social media is mainly something I do as part of my business; I don't want to or need to share my life.

I love reading, I love learning, I love being a mum, I love running three businesses, but a glam lifestyle? No.

I did a talk a few years back on Comparison Syndrome. How we look at others and their happy, sociable, perfect lives and then compare ourselves to these images and comments putting ourselves down and thinking we are not good enough.

I don't need to take endless selfies to show the world how good (or bad) I look, I don't have to stand at the playground telling everyone how wonderful my children are, I don't need to market my business by saying how many figures I make each month, and I don't need to post pictures of my food trying to convince myself and everyone around me I am a healthy eater.

I am an ordinary, hard-working, slightly (OK not so slightly) over-weight, 36-year-old mum that loves watching films, walking the dog, and getting her house in order. Superwoman/man was not a working parent, their outfits make that clear from the offset—you cannot play football, tie shoelaces, walk the dog, or shop in that outfit.

- Love being "ordinary"
- Love the life you have
- And don't compare yourself to others—they often only show you what they want you to see.

Getting in your own way, filling your head with "ifs and buts," and waiting for tomorrow can hold you back, but often, it is only us that get in our own way, however much we look to blame other parts of our lives, and as long as we can keep shifting the blame elsewhere, we always have a reason to stay right where we are, letting our own thoughts and actions get right in the way of where we want to be, in the safe protection of ifs and buts.

Say No

I know, I know, you want to say no, you really do, but a parent from school has asked you to help with a social event, your boss wants the report in on the same day, the kids need new shoes, and your partner has this "big proj-ect" on at work where they really need some space at the minute, your par-ents want to come for dinner, your friends want to pop round for drinks as they haven't seen you in ages and you promised yourself some "me time."

What do you say no to?

Honestly, what do you say no to?

On a scale of 1 to 10, when you think of how much people will judge you, or how guilty you will feel about letting them down if you said no to any of the above, where do you sit?

Top end of the scale?

So, you say yes, you run yourself ragged and the only thing you don't have time for is your "me time," because clearly you are not a priority. You do everything you said you would and more, because more people asked for help and now you are too busy, too frazzled, and too worried about being judged to say no or ask for help and all you hear yourself saying as you sit in yet more traffic is "If I hadn't said yes to......," or "Yes I know I'm late again but......" You fill in the blanks.

Take some time, stop, write down everything that is in your head, prioritize it, and say no, even if just to one thing.

Try these tips:

- Be clear on your own priorities before you say yes
- Remember "no" is a complete sentence
- Keep it simple—you don't owe anyone any explanations
- Don't answer right away—take some time to consider your options
- Provide an alternative—only if you want to

Getting out of your own way yet?

Dissociate

I want to tell you a quick story ...

Once upon a time a there was a woman who judged the way people looked, how they spoke, and how they interacted with others. She went to a coffee shop, sat quietly for an hour and during this time watched people as they walked past, as they entered the coffee shop, and as they interacted with others.

She noticed her thoughts and let them go (Dissociated). When she reflected on her thoughts that evening, she noticed that what she had been judging others on were the negative thought patterns she had about herself. She was conscious of her weight, conscious of how she looked, and conscious of how she spoke. When she learned to accept herself for who she was, she became more accepting of those around her and less judgmental.

How do you feel reading that?

It's a true story, about me.

My Mum had always (until recently) been uncomfortable with her weight and how others perceived her and this was passed on to me, with me believing that I couldn't wear certain things because of how I would be judged by others.

What I learned:

- Be comfortable with who you are
- If ever you judge people ask yourself what it is within you that you need to work on
- Reflection is a powerful tool

The "F" Word—How to Overcome Fear

How often has fear held you back in your life?

Where could you be now if you had found excitement over fear and gone for it?

I can't remember who said it, or in what context, but many years ago, I was told that fear and excitement triggered the same physical reaction in our bodies and that the only way to differentiate between the two was how we saw them in our heads. It was sometime later before I put this into action.

A couple of months after starting my first business I was on my way to deliver a talk to a women-in-business forum, arranged by a large bank. I had talked many times before and loved being on stage, sharing stories and tips, and was delighted to have been invited to this particular event.

I had not long left my house and was driving in my car when I started getting butterflies in my stomach; my heart was racing, my breathing becoming more intense, and I felt the fear kicking in.

While I had spoken many times before, it had been on behalf of my employers. The large corporations that paid me a wage in return for hard work, and I had always had their brand behind me. This time, it was just me. Me, my business, and my brand. No large company, no large brand, just me.

I began to feel terrified, realizing these physical feelings were fear and I considered turning the car round. Then my intellectual mind took over, told me I was not going home and that I would be fine by the time I got on stage.

But, what if I wasn't? What if I fell to pieces? I must go home, I can't do it.

It was then, like a bolt out of nowhere, that I remembered fear and excitement had the same physical reaction, allegedly!

I started telling myself I was excited. I told myself this was an exciting opportunity for me to prove I didn't need a big brand behind me. I could do this, I would do this, and it was really exciting to be asked to do a talk this early on in setting up my business.

I arrived at the event, prepared, excited, and ready to go, calmed my breathing, stood up, delivered my talk, and received the most amazing feedback. I had done it, I had actually done it. I felt proud, if a little exhausted, but I had done it.

Think of a time where fear made you turn the car around?

When have you done something you didn't think you could just by the power of positive thinking?

Top Tips

- Tell fear it is excitement—and believe it
- Aim high, think big—the worst you can do is fail
- How you choose to feel is your decision—make the right choice

PART IV
Case Studies/Stories

Case Study 1—Tania Rose

Tania Rose works as a coach for singers and performers. Let's look at one of her stories about two singers waiting for an audition.

Sally is nervous. That's what she's been telling herself all day ("God, I'm sooo nervous. I wish I wasn't nervous. I can't handle this nervousness!"). She sits in the waiting area to be called, wringing her hands, trying to breathe in and out like her mum used to tell her before the school play would start as a kid. She's is trying to relax, tries to distract herself from even thinking about her cold hands and her body's shaking by disengaging from the whole idea. "Don't think about it," she tells herself. "Think about other things." She withdraws within herself in an attempt to escape.

Jen is also waiting to be called in. She's been bubbling over most of the day. She was so excited this morning that she went for a short run before she got ready, just to settle herself. She's been thinking about the audition all day, humming out her songs to herself, playing it over in her mind as her butterflies flutter away in her stomach, but she's been telling herself, "I'm soooooo excited! This is going to be so great. I'm so lucky to be here!" She didn't believe herself at first, tempted to call it "nerves," but she resisted. In the waiting area she feels the excitement level increasing. She paces the floor, bouncing on the spot every now and then to discharge her adrenaline, and keeps herself focused and in a positive state of mind. Her body is doing the same things that Sally's is, but Jen keeps moving and keeps up her positive mind-speak.

The two have totally different experiences with their audition. Sally has spent so much of her time trying to distance herself from thinking about the audition that she appears disinterested in it. She has been trying to keep her body so still by attempting to relax that as soon as she goes to sing, her cells fire up from the buildup of chemicals and she loses vocal control. She gets really down on herself and has given up before she's even halfway through. She leaves in tears, gutted by another sense of failure.

Jen bounds into the room, and her energy is immediately obvious. She's been releasing her adrenaline all day, so she maintains a lot of vocal control. She brings to her audition a sense of excitement and passion, and though she makes mistakes, she keeps positive and moves on, so well in fact that some of the panel don't even notice her errors. She leaves with a feeling of success.

The flight or fight response is our body's way of preparing us for engagement. Whether you call it excitement or nervousness, it's the same physical thing. Chemicals get released into our cells to prepare them with optimum power and strength, and are there to save your life. One of the mistakes people make when they have these feelings is to try and calm them down, but our body is geared up for battle, not for meditation.

If you focus instead on releasing the pressure physically (jump up and down, run around the block, etc.) and tell yourself over and over how excited you are (even if at first you don't believe it), you can make a huge difference to your experience. You can then learn to USE that amazing zing and turn it into an opportunity to deliver in a way you can't when you're in your comfort zone.

Harnessing this energy instead of denying it can turn a good delivery into something quite remarkable.

Are fear and excitement the same? Try it out for yourself, and you be the judge.

Case Study 2—Knowing Your Value

Just as we believe our life begins when we get the thing we *need*, we also look for validation from others to determine our worth. We look for a certain salary to be earned, for people to pay a price for our service or product, or for our business to be worth a certain amount of money.

I don't know if you ever saw it, but a year or so ago there was a campaign advertising a job for people to apply online. You had to be multiskilled and able to work long hours. When the shortlisted applicants were interviewed they were told they would receive no pay, no holiday, and be required to work 24/7, 365 days a year for the rest of their lives. Nobody wanted the job. Yet many of us are already doing it. It's called being a Mum.

It's time we let go of putting a price on our head. You are priceless.

And while you're forgetting about the money, forget about the likes, shares, and followers that you have or want or need. And the haters—forget about the haters.

Let's break this down a little.

For hundreds of years, thousands even, perhaps even since the beginning of time, people have been judging other people.

Now, however, we place our own value on our own head. But we don't always seem sure what that value is. We look in the mirror and see worthless. We look at our career, our house, our bank balance, or some other area of our life and we tell ourselves we are not enough, or believe the hype from everyone around us.

When we start work in our teens (and I only mean part-time work, not child labor) or early 20s, we value ourselves on an hourly rate. This seems fine to start with. We do work and we receive money in return. Until we decide that the job we are being paid to do is now worth more than the hourly rate we started on. The job hasn't changed, but we have. We have decided we are worth more than the job we are doing. We decide we are worth more per hour or more per year.

If, like me, you've left the corporate life behind you and have started your own business, you may have a product or service to sell and you start to base your price on how much time it will take to deliver, or to incorporate manufacturing costs, or to be in line with your competition, and so on. As your business grows, and your money grows, so too you believe, does your worth.

We've all seen the rich lists published. Richard Branson is worth $X million. J. K. Rowling is now no longer classed as a billionaire as she gave money to charity. Does this make her worth less?

Then, aside from the money, we value ourselves on how many friends or followers we have. How many likes, shares, retweets, or comments we get. The online world is getting louder and with this our "value" of self-worth is decreasing. Even with the publishing of this book, the number of connections I have will be viewed far more important than the quality of the writing because the connections are likely to buy the book, which, of course, equals money.

We post selfies of ourselves looking our best, woes of our bad days, and pictures of our meals in the hope that "lots" of people will like it, comment on it and share it to make us feel worthy. This week I've removed myself from Facebook so I can focus on the writing of this book and other work projects. I love people, but I need to shut off every now and again to focus on what's important. I don't think any publisher will be pleased to hear this news!

Then we have the opinions of others that we value ourselves on, and this is where things can reach rock bottom for us, especially if this is where we hold our value most. It is here, where we can stop living. Where we can freeze, stop taking action, feel worthless and no good, and need a shopping trip to make us feel better about ourselves because there is something wrong with us that makes us feel less complete.

Every one of my clients has grown. Some much more than they hoped, some in ways they never imagined. All have grown, all flourished, all flown.

I've always received lovely feedback whether it's been from clients or a member of their family or from an audience member at a talk I have given or a webinar I have hosted. Sometimes there's lots of great feedback, sometimes just one person.

Earlier this year a friend of mine was round having a coffee and a catch up and we got to the point where the conversation went back two years. For two years she had been in the same place, and while we had talked about it and I had been to events with her and given advice and support and suggestions, she didn't make the transition, something was holding her back.

So I offered a day of my time to her, which she told me she couldn't afford, but I really felt I needed to help her and I gifted her the day. My choice, of course. I wanted to see her move forward and from a selfish point of view I wanted to hear about her successes instead of her obstacles when we met.

The day arrived and I went to her house, even paying for my own taxi as she was unable to pick me up due to car problems and I was still a nondriver at the time. She didn't seem particularly ready, prepared, or engaged, but we set to work and we carried on until her husband arrived home.

I saw and heard the breakthroughs she experienced that day, so I was shocked when, as I was leaving, she disclosed she had never done any personal development before and didn't understand why people would pay for it.

Since our day together she has grown in confidence and ability, found a new focus, started a second business and personal brand, and attended other personal development workshops that she has openly told me she paid thousands of pounds for. She has flourished and grown, and while it's not all down to me, I know the change and shift she had that day and how I helped her unlock what she already inside of her which has allowed her to go on and achieve great success and she has done all of that on her own.

I could have let her comment get to me. I could have been bothered by the fact that she sees her success as nothing to do with me at all. I'm not. All I did and all I do with anyone I work with is create the space to unlock their potential, and if she couldn't see the value in that, that's totally up to her.

When we place our value on the comments and opinions of others, good or bad, positive or negative, we lose our own self-worth. If my value in myself is only present when I receive good and positive comments, then surely that would mean my value decreases when I receive comments that are poor or negative.

I know the value I provide my clients so that they can find their wings and fly, and often to them, the outcomes are priceless. I also know the value I place on my friends and my family and the value they get from me in return and none of this is to do with money.

While I would happily work with all of my clients for free, I don't. First, I have bills of my own to pay and second, when you pay for me, you don't just pay for the time I have worked with you or for the online material, you are paying for my experience, for all I have learned over the years, for all I know, for all I am, and you can then take what works for you and put it to your own use.

Remember also, that not everyone will like you and that's ok.

Don't let anyone determine your value or your worth. Be true to yourself. Know that you are valuable, priceless even, and start living.

You are already of value.

Case Study 3—Your Dreams Won't Work Unless You Do

As a child did you dream of what you would be when you grew up?

Dancer? Singer? Doctor? Nurse? Lawyer? On Top of the Pops? Nobel Prize Winner? TV Presenter? Famous? Writer? Model? Astronaut? Vet? Teacher?

How did that turn out?

I don't remember at what ages, but at some point in my life I wanted to be Madonna, a nurse, a midwife, a teacher, a solicitor, Matilda (Roald Dahl), a dancer (from Fame), in Cats, famous (so I could be on Comic Relief and help the kids in Africa), Alan Sugar, Richard Branson, Darcey Bussell, and the Queen.

Never did I dream of being a management trainee for a retailer, an HR Director, or running my own businesses.

At some point in life my dreams changed, maybe because I outgrew my idea, perhaps something else took my fancy, and in most cases because I was told it would never happen (like being Madonna, Richard Branson, Darcey Bussell, Alan Sugar, and the Queen), or that it only happens to some people.

You, I, we are some people. Whatever you want to do, you have all you need right here, right now to get you there. Unless, of course, you want to be someone else, you can only be *you*.

I'm not going to tell you to limit your dreams or think of something more realistic but I do want you to consider:

Will I *still* be happy when I make it? (*not* will it make me happy, you need to do that on your own first)

Will it light me up?

Will I still feel alive?

And I want you to consider these three things because if you're not happy now, why will you be then? If you're not lit up now, why will you be then? If you don't feel alive now, when?

Dreams and ambitions are great to have, but you can live without them. You have all you need right now. What will your dreams provide you that you don't already have?

Sometimes our dreams can be a burden. We see it on TV all the time. "I wanted to be a singer all my life so I went on X-Factor, failed and now I feel like my life is over" and if you struggle to see what you have in your life and that your life has already begun, your dream can become a nightmare.

And it becomes a nightmare because you think that without that one thing you are not enough, or that you can't live without it, or you can't be happy without it.

Dreams take work. Dreams won't work unless you do.

Dreaming of being an artist won't work unless you pick up a paintbrush.

Dreaming of being a photographer involves picking up a camera.

Dreaming of writing, being a CEO, running your own business, surfing, sculpting, chefing, drawing, being a parent, teacher, astronaut, runner, athlete, model, actress, radio-presenter, TV host, journalist, designer, marketer, happy, healthy, wealthy, whatever you dream of, it takes work.

I pushed and worked hard for my entire career. I juggled promotions with my marriage and motherhood, and once on the ladder, I dreamed of being an HR Director. When I got there I wasn't happy.

I then started dreaming of having my own business and when I got there I wasn't happy.

When I dreamed of being happy, I found it. I was happy.

I didn't have to buy anything or be anything that I wasn't already. In a matter of days, I was happy. My dream came true.

From that day on I have found happiness in every day. It took work, it takes work, it took courage and every day I still work at being happy. I have to choose happiness on gray days. Sometimes I have to look for happiness, but it's always there inside me. In the small things. Not in the job or the bank balance.

We have to act if we want our dreams to come true because Action Changes Things. The law of attraction (LOA) will have us believe that if we think if we can have it, but it's more complicated than that.

I didn't think this book into existence, I had to write it. You can't think yourself a millionaire, you have to work for it or at least buy a ticket to be in with a chance of winning the lottery. But if you are waiting for the law of attraction to make your dreams come true, you could be waiting for a long time.

Yes, you have to be in alignment with your dreams and yes you have to raise your vibration, but you also have to feel it. And from my experience of LOA, you only get what you want when you realize you don't need it.

Let's say you do dream of winning the lottery. You try and align yourself and you buy a ticket, but you don't win. What's the reason you want to win? To help others? For security? For financial freedom? Something else? The *reason* you want it is the part to align yourself to, and that may not come with the outcome of a lottery win.

There are other ways to help others and to find security and to gain financial freedom; and if you truly align the *why* to the energy, you will find the right outcome, but it will still take work. Perhaps not a lot of work, but work. It takes action, it takes commitment, and it takes energy.

So define your dream, work out why it's a dream, align it to your purpose, and go for it. Start living, start creating miracles.

Case Study 4—Walking on Broken Glass

I had always wanted to walk on hot coals; it wasn't a burning desire but every time I saw a fire walk advertised I would tell myself I'll do it one day.

While recording a series of podcasts, I interviewed two women who had both attended a four-day fire-walking intensive, a weekend of extreme empowerment, just a few miles from my home with the guy who had taught Tony Robbins. I didn't interview them because of the fire walking, but of course, because they had done it, it came up in conversation.

Listening to both of their stories and how much they had learned about themselves over the four days, I looked into doing it myself. The days of the training didn't fit for me but the promise of doing it soon moved up my list of things to do.

A couple of weeks later I was speaking at a business show delivering a seminar and a keynote talk. The seminar on Mindset and the keynote about The F Word—Recognizing and Overcoming Fear. I'd been working a lot with fear over the last few years, researching and delivering talks and workshops, and I sat to write my talk and prepare my presentation, although something felt different.

This talk wasn't going to be based on research or anything I had used for my previous talks or workshops. This talk was about my own journey with fear. I kept trying to take it back to everything I had done before but my gut kept putting the talk back to me.

I had 45 minutes in which to present my journey and that didn't seem long enough, so still I kept pulling it back to the research. It wasn't working.

I crafted my talk as a timeline. The ages and milestones where fear had crept up on me, jumped out at me, and been present and what I thought and felt the driving factors had been at each stage. Some of the big things, the terrible things, the hard things—I tried to leave out, but my gut told me to include everything, warts and all. I kept trying to edit these out but I was being pulled toward including them. I gave in and put in all of the points. As I read it, back it was hard. It felt raw and I felt vulnerable but I was pleased to have got it all out of my head and onto paper. And as I read it, I realized that without the warts, it was like Snow White with only five dwarfs—an incomplete story.

The day of the talks arrived. I had been picked up from home in the morning by one of the other speakers as I still wasn't driving and we arrived in plenty of time. I met face to face for the first time one of the fire-walking interviewees who was also speaking that day, and in addition to her talks she had a stand with a glass walk. "Oh great, I'll give that a go later," I said to her first thing in the morning.

Later in the day I had an excuse for not doing it there and then. I had calls to make, e-mails to respond to, lunch to eat, people to talk to, and of course my seminar and talk to prepare for. I delivered the seminar and some of the people then said they would be coming to hear my keynote later that afternoon.

As the day went on I was getting more and more worried about my talk. Not the presenting—I love speaking on stage (even as a total introvert)—but the content of my talk was worrying me. Perhaps I still had time to edit it and leave out the warts.

I wanted my talk to be engaging and for the audience to take something from it and I didn't think the content would do that or be relevant to anyone if I left it as it was. This was a business show; what did my personal journey have to do with any of it. I had a plan. I would only talk about the relevant bits. But I didn't know the audience and I couldn't guess which parts would be relevant to them. What should I do?

Well, I delivered the talk, warts and all. I was vulnerable, I was brave, and I had battled another fear that day. A fear of being judged on my past. At the end of the talk two women ran up to me, giving thanks, well done's and telling me how inspirational and amazing I was and I said thank you as I stood there knowing I had done something to make myself feel lighter and to set myself free. Not only had I told my story, but it felt as though I had healed that bit more and closed wounds from the past that I didn't know still needed healing.

I had done it. I felt good.

I went back into the exhibition arena to find the friend who was giving me a lift home and to confirm the time we would be leaving. We had about 30 minutes until we left.

I moved over to the glass-walk, the "guardian" of the glass was delivering her final seminar, she was running over and would be with me very soon, I was told by her wife and partner. The excuses started to flow from my mouth freely. Don't worry; I'm leaving soon; I'll do it next time. The clock was ticking and my lift home was my get-out-of-jail-free card.

Home-time was coming ever closer; the seminar continued; today was not my day, but still I waited. My friend was then ready to leave and she came over to where I was standing. I told her we could go if she was ready, she told me she was fine to wait. My get-out-of-jail-free card vanished.

It wasn't so much the walking on glass barefoot that was bothering me; it was this feeling churning in my stomach, of failing, of being the center of attention, of people watching me and judging me. I had just done all of that on stage though and bared my soul in the process, so what was the issue?

I felt fat—what's that got to do with glass?

I don't like my feet—they will be on the glass, nobody cares about your feet!

I won't be able to do it—yes you will!

So I told myself it was all in my head. Ego was back, I told her I was doing it and I actually started to feel quite excited. The time came; I kicked off my shoes, listened to the instructions I was being given, and there I was—I was walking on broken glass.

I had a little wobble in the middle when a mountain of glass came from nowhere underfoot and made me a little unstable, but I found my balance again and in less than a minute I had done it. I felt liberated. I felt free. I had grown.

Something in me changed that day. All of the research, everything I had overcome from my past, now all felt insignificant, yet I knew it had helped me. My actions and my thoughts had helped me achieve things that had worried me. My life didn't start that day—I was already alive and kicking—but I started that day with a new page, more clarity, more confidence, more control, and more self-belief. I had walked my talk, and not for the first time, but it was the first time I had done it on glass.

What do you need to walk on to help you start a blank page today?

Case Study 5—Focus on Feeling

Karen and I had been working together for a couple of weeks to help increase her confidence at work. Over the last few months she had felt herself on a downward spiral and didn't know how to pick herself back up.

Our first two sessions had gone well and Karen was visibly more confident in the way she was speaking, her posture, the way she carried herself—she already looked like a new person.

At today's session Karen shared with me that she was going in for an operation in two weeks' time; she was terrified, but hoped it would take a lot of the pain she had been feeling. We explored this in more detail and she opened up to say that she felt the pain was related to stress caused by her manager. We spoke about choices.

The operation went ahead as planned, the recovery time was longer than anticipated, and we had four weeks of e-mail contact but no sessions.

When we got together Karen seemed to have taken a step backward. She appeared timid and was emotional and fearful of returning to work. The break had made her realize that she needed a new job, but she had to stick with it for now.

She was due to be having a meeting with her manager the next day, but was worried that she would need to pick up exactly where she left off and she didn't want to go back to working 60 hours a week, picking up the slack of her boss and having her boss ignore her request for an additional team member.

We focused on the meeting. Karen said she knew exactly what she wanted to say, but that she also knew what her boss would say and so she knew the meeting would be a waste of time.

In reality, while we can think we know what is going to happen, we never truly know how other people will react or what they will say. And if we spend too long trying to work out what other people will say, what they will do, and how they will behave we will tie ourselves up in knots.

Instead of focusing on the script of the conversation, we focused on how Karen wanted to feel at the end of the meeting.

Her face lit up. "If I could feel calm it would be a godsend."

We talked about some practical steps and mindset techniques that would help Karen to feel calm by the end of the meeting.

She called me immediately afterward and told me she felt amazing. She had focused on keeping calm, was able to say exactly what she needed to say, and her boss actually agreed to start recruiting for some extra help.

Case Study 6—I Am Carefree

Alex and I met for a discovery session in the lobby of a beautiful London hotel. He had been given my details by a friend and we were meeting to see if we could work together.

I treat this session as a coaching session; it's like test-driving a car. How do you know if you actually want to buy if you don't experience the ride for yourself?

Alex worked as a Finance Director for a large consultancy firm and wasn't getting on with his boss. Everything felt it was crashing around him. He wanted to take a sabbatical and go away and do some voluntary work abroad but didn't feel he could do this on his own.

He went on to explain that he had always been a worrier. Since he was a child, his parents, his siblings, his teachers, everyone had told him he was a worrier; it was part of who he was. And it was now impacting on his work. He felt he couldn't do anything right, he was worried about the performance of his team (which, it transpired, wasn't a problem), and he was shying away from having conversations with colleagues because he was worried what the CEO would say to him if he had to take a firm stance.

I asked him how he would like to feel. He said he wanted to be able to stop worrying. I asked him how he would feel about being carefree instead of a worrier. Everything about him changed. His shoulders softened, his frown turned to a smile, and he looked less guarded.

"Carefree, that would be amazing."

I asked him how he would feel about replacing the word "worrier" with the word "carefree" and if this would work for him. "Yes."

Alex and I met again a few weeks later. He looked different, he sounded different. He had met with his boss and talked about his concerns, he had met with his colleagues and "laid it on the line," his family had noticed how different he was and he had even booked his sabbatical abroad and asked if we would continue to work together while he was there.

Alex is now back in the UK as a Finance Director in a large corporate-finance company. He is confident, happy, and carefree.

PART V

Mindset Tips and Tools

Your Perfect Day Mindset

I mentioned earlier on that we would map out your perfect day to help you map out the life you want to help you on the right path, and to do that, we are going now to map out your perfect day.

This is your perfect average day and by that I mean to create the life you desire and the future you deserve, what would your day-to-day life be like, the perfect day every day in the future?

We will break this down into three categories, Planning, Deeper Stuff, and The Really Deep Stuff.

Note your thoughts down to the following questions and then we will map out your strategy for action.

Planning

Where will you live?

What will your house look like?

What time will you wake up?

What will you do in the morning?

(It is so important to see these things in detail.)

What will you have for breakfast?

What thoughts will you be having in the morning?

How will you spend the first half of the day?

What will you have for lunch?

Who will you eat with?

What will your friends be like?

What will you talk about?

Deeper Stuff

What will you do for personal fulfillment?

What life purpose will you strive toward?

What work will you be doing?

Who will you be working with?

What hours will you work?

What will you enjoy about your work?

The Really Deep Stuff

What is your relationship like?

What do you do for family time?

Winding down?

What do you do in the evenings?

Who do you do it with?

Where?

Thoughts before going to sleep?

Questions for Success

The following questions will help you to gain a deeper understanding of yourself and your mindset.

The deeper the answers the more effective the results will be.

The questions are:

- Who am I?
- What is my vision for the future?

- What are my strengths?
- What do I want even more of?
- What are the main priorities in my life right now?
- What are the three biggest priorities in my life right now?
- Where am I focusing my time right now?
- What will I say no to right now?
- Knowing who I am and where I want to be in the future, how will I use my strengths to focus on my priorities as they are today?
- Knowing who I am and where I want to be in the future, what do I need to focus on to develop myself and achieve my vision?
- What is the one question I don't want to be asked right now?
- Where is my mindset holding me back in my life right now?

Mindset Techniques

1. EARN Your Leadership—At the end of each day score yourself on these four areas from 0 to 5. Top athletes score 17 and above. E = Exercise, A = Attitude, R = Rejuvenation, N = Nutrition. Your mental and physical well-being work in unison; don't neglect any of them.

2. POWER Up—At the start of every day answer these six questions to set your intentions and get you in the right mindset for the day ahead.
   1. What was the best part of yesterday?
   2. What did you learn?
   3. What value do you intend to operate from today?
   4. What action do you intend to do today to honor your values?
   5. What will the desired outcome be?
   6. What will you enjoy about your life today?

3. Interview Questions—Ask at least five people these questions to understand how others see you. You can ask face-to-face, by phone, or by e-mail—it's up to you. Don't say anything other than thank you when you get the feedback. Feedback is a gift, treat it as one!
   1. What can you count on me for?
   2. What can you not count on me for?

3. What is the skill or talent I am crazy good at?
4. If you could give me one piece of advice, what would it be?

Mindset Tips

- You have chosen your career and your job—Love Mondays, even if you have to fake it for a while.
- Find ways to reduce your workload and your stress—If you can't, try some mindfulness, breathing techniques, or increase your exercise to release your happy hormones.
- Think back to why you chose your career/job in the first place—What did you say and do at your interview to prove you deserved the job? How passionate were you? Reignite that passion.
- If you have lost your passion—Move on!
- Be clear on your vision and do all you can to stay focused.
- Surround yourself with energy angels—People and tasks that fill you with energy.
- Limit the time you spend with energy vampires—People and tasks that drain you of energy. Ideally you want a ratio of 3:1, angels to vampires.
- Know what it takes to make your business work.
- Know what your clients want.
- Know where you need to adapt and grow—Take steps to make it happen.
- Identify where you need help—and then get it.
- Look into yourself and be clear on what you are trying to create before engaging others to help.
- Take time out to relax and switch off.
- Remember that being busy is not the same as being productive.
- Be grateful.
- Celebrate success.
- Carve your diary into 90-minute blocks.
- Stay focused.
- Have fun!

About the Author

Kelly Swingler lives in Peterborough, UK, with her partner Mick, sons Callum and Robert, step-sons Cameron and Harry, and pets Bowser the Bulldog and Robert's Bearded Dragons, Soy and Wasabi.

Founder of Chrysalis Consulting, she supports people, teams, and companies in changing mindsets to transform performance.

Before starting Chrysalis Consulting, Kelly worked in HR, L&D, and OD, latterly as an HR Director, and was appointed as the UK's youngest HR Director, according to the Chartered Institute of Personnel and Development (CIPD), UK.

Passionate about developing people and helping them unlock their potential, Kelly loves her work and her clients and is building a future doing work she loves while enjoying the freedom it gives her to continue to learn, grow and develop and spend more time with family and friends.

Kelly is a Chartered Member of the CIPD and holds a wealth of HR, L&D, and OD qualifications, as well as being a qualified Executive Coach, Hypnotherapist, and Psychotherapist in addition to her BSc in Psychology. She is currently undertaking a PhD in Organizational Change.

Writing, Yoga, films, and music are what Kelly enjoys in her spare time when she is not spending time with family and friends. She loves being outdoors and visits Ibiza as often as she can to spend time with her brother and sister.

Find out more at www.chrysalis-consulting.co.uk

Index

OTHER TITLES IN THE HUMAN RESOURCE MANAGEMENT AND ORGANIZATIONAL BEHAVIOR COLLECTION

- *The Illusion of Inclusion: Global Inclusion, Unconscious Bias, and the Bottom Line* by Helen Turnbull
- *On All Cylinders: The Entrepreneur's Handbook* by Ron Robinson
- *Employee LEAPS: Leveraging Engagement by Applying Positive Strategies* by Kevin E. Phillips
- *Making Human Resource Technology Decisions: A Strategic Perspective* by Janet H. Marler and Sandra L. Fisher
- *Feet to the Fire: How to Exemplify And Create The Accountability That Creates Great Companies* By Lorraine A. Moore
- *HR Analytics and Innovations in Workforce Planning* By Tony Miller
- *Deconstructing Management Maxims, Volume I: A Critical Examination of Conventional Business Wisdom* by Kevin Wayne
- *Deconstructing Management Maxims, Volume II: A Critical Examination of Conventional Business Wisdom* by Kevin Wayne
- *The Real Me: Find and Express Your Authentic Self* by Mark Eyre
- *Across the Spectrum: What Color Are You?* by Stephen Elkins-Jarrett
- *The Human Resource Professional's Guide to Change Management: Practical Tools and Techniques to Enact Meaningful and Lasting Organizational Change* by Melanie J. Peacock
- *Tough Calls: How to Move Beyond Indecision and Good Intentions* by Linda D. Henman

Announcing the Business Expert Press Digital Library

Concise e-books business students need for classroom and research

This book can also be purchased in an e-book collection by your library as

- a one-time purchase,
- that is owned forever,
- allows for simultaneous readers,
- has no restrictions on printing, and
- can be downloaded as PDFs from within the library community.

Our digital library collections are a great solution to beat the rising cost of textbooks. E-books can be loaded into their course management systems or onto students' e-book readers.
The **Business Expert Press** digital libraries are very affordable, with no obligation to buy in future years. For more information, please visit **www.businessexpertpress.com/librarians**. To set up a trial in the United States, please email **sales@businessexpertpress.com**.